LITTLE BLUES BOOK

LITTLE
BLUES
BOOK

BRIAN ROBERTSON

ILLUSTRATIONS BY R. CRUMB

Algonquin Books of Chapel Hill 1996

Published by
ALGONQUIN BOOKS OF CHAPEL HILL
Post Office Box 2225
Chapel Hill, North Carolina 27515-2225

a division of
WORKMAN PUBLISHING
708 Broadway
New York, New York 10003

For permission to use quotations from copyrighted works, grateful acknowledgment is made to the holders of copyright, publishers, or representatives named on pages (173–74), which constitute an extension of the copyright page.

LIBRARY OF CONGRESS CATALOGING-IN-PUBLICATION DATA
Little blues book / [compiled] by Brian Robertson; illustrations by R. Crumb.
   p. cm.
  Includes bibliographical references.
  ISBN 1-56512-137-6
  1. Blues (Music)—Texts. 2. Blues (Music)—Miscellanea.
I. Robertson, Brian, 1951–   .
ML54.6.L47 1996 <Case>
782.42'1643'0268—dc20   96-19571
                                      CIP
                                     MN

10 9 8 7 6 5 4 3 2

*This book is especially for the musicians
I've played with throughout the years
and for the people who have been there
to listen and to inspire.*

You take one man's heart and make another man live
You even go to the moon and come back thrilled
Why, you can crush any country in a matter of weeks
But it don't make sense you can't make peace.

—"It Don't Make Sense (You Can't Make Peace)"
by WILLIE DIXON

CONTENTS

OPENING REFRAIN BY WILLIE DIXON

People always come up and ask me what is my favorite song out of all the hundreds of songs that I've written. Most everybody figures I'll call some song that made a lot of money or that one of the rock bands did that got my name out there to the public. Frankly, it's a song I wrote some years ago that I had on this Pausa recording: "It Don't Make Sense (You Can't Make Peace)."

I did "It Don't Make Sense" many times on the stage and the audience always was spellbound when we did it. The place would come to a complete standstill, big or small, but somehow we never did get much radio play on that.

The blues are supposed to put thoughts in the minds of people but any time you get involved with something that's really good for the people, you can't get much publicity on it because everybody is banking more on trying to get financial rewards on a thing than they are on the wisdom of it. The blues was made for wisdom but they'd rather play the record they know that some kid is going to dance to and buy whether the song has wisdom or not.

This wisdom of the blues can be used all through life and that's why most blues songs are written as a statement of wisdom. I'd say that from 95% up to 99% of the world believes that it don't make sense you can't make peace.

It couldn't make sense you can't make peace if you want to

make peace. You can make anything else you want on earth—the best plane, the biggest ships, everything to fight with—but suppose we spend just half the time and amount of money making peace that we have spent making war? There wouldn't be a mouth on earth that wouldn't be fed and nobody would have to suffer.

Out of all the things we did and made on earth, regardless of how we use them, it don't make sense unless we have peace enough that we can enjoy the world. God made man the greatest of all the animals but you ain't satisfied with that. You think you're smarter and you have to get to killing each other. For what? It's all vanity, anyway.

The wisdom and knowledge of the blues are these facts of life. I feel that if the proper songs get to the various people of the world, it helps their mind to concentrate on what's going on in the world and this will give you a better communication. That's the real meaning and the real good of the blues, a better education and understanding among all people.

The blues being the true facts of life, we know it has been a fact of life that the people in the world have always made whatever they wanted. In making the many things of the world, we've made everything but peace. If you accept the wisdom of the blues, we can definitely have peace.

—from *I Am the Blues: The Willie Dixon Story*
by Willie Dixon with Don Snowden

THE VOICE OF THE BLUES:
AN INTRODUCTION

Stop, look and listen—I hear somebody calling me. It's the voice of the blues calling me back to my used to be.
IRENE SCRUGGS,
"Voice of the Blues"

Let's get one thing straight—I'm not here to explain the blues. Just the opposite. The blues are here to explain me.

And they'll explain a lot about you, too.

And about life.

But don't take my word for it. Instead, take the words of some of the masters of the blues—stories and lyrics pulled from their performances over the last seventy-plus years. A walk through this book is a chance to ramble through the varied flavor of the blues and to discover a voice that speaks deeply and profoundly—yet simply—straight to the heart.

When I was sixteen and everybody else had intense Beatlemania, there were only two albums on the shelf next to my record player. The first was a record of the wonderful sitar music of Ravi Shankar, the beginning of my long-standing love of Eastern philosophy and music. The second album was a double-record set by Lightnin' Hopkins that had been played so often it crackled, sounding as if it might have been recorded during a forest fire. It was from that Lightnin' Hopkins record that I learned to pick slow blues on an old guitar. As I grew up in Houston, I was able to hear and see legends like Lightnin' Hopkins, Mance Lipscomb, Juke Boy Bonner, and countless others. As I got older, I actually found myself playing on stage with some of the blues masters in coffeehouses and bars. The blues became a part of me, and I've been playing them on stages around the country for a quarter of a century.

There was something about the blues that hit me from the very beginning. I still can't say exactly what it is that weaves that distinct and powerful spell, but I can tell you this—after two divorces, miles of travel, two hundred nights a year on stage, and some forty-five years of living, I know that no matter what I'm feeling I can point to a line from this book and say, "Well, *there* it is! That's *exactly* how I feel!"

After all, the blues shares with poetry the basic quality of offering a skillfully condensed and intensified "snapshot" of an experience. The essence of the music is simple and direct, as are the lyrics, and for that reason it seems to me the great blues singers are America's Zen masters. They are men and women deeply in touch with the here and now who tap into the very essence of human experience, longing, and loss through the simplicity and direct truths of their songs. The feelings in the blues are not limited to sadness, for a person can find undisputed joy in the music and can benefit from an attitude that speaks and sings of a kind of cosmic comedy. In the blues, the line between tragedy and comedy is frequently blurred. Willie Dixon explained it all by saying, "You can have the blues one day because your woman went away. Then you can have the blues the next day because she came back."

In compiling this book, I completely abandoned earlier efforts to simply list or group lyrics together and began again totally from scratch, deciding this time to start with some of the wonderful stories and anecdotes about bluesmen and -women. From that, I started selecting songs that spoke to the spirit of the blues as revealed in the stories of the lives of those who had made the music. I chose to follow the quotes with the names of the singers I first heard sing or speak the lyrics — the musician listed might not even be the first or the most famous to deliver the quoted lines. In many cases the songs and lyrics are from collections of outtakes and alternative versions and simply bear the title "Unknown" on the recordings and, for that reason, in this book as well. Some were quoted to me and attributed to a certain blues singer, whose name I have attached to them.

So what are the blues? In thinking about that question, I remembered hearing Joseph Campbell talk extensively about "the joyful participation in the sorrows of the world." That, I think, is the central essence of the blues experience: its honest look at who we are, where we're going, and what we've done in our lives.

The more I play the blues and the more I listen to them, the deeper they seem to take me. The lyrics themselves are often drawn from a vast pool of wisdom set in rhyme, or perhaps it is more accurate to say that this "pool" is a great river whose source is shrouded in mystery. We may never know the exact origins of the blues form, the names of those who first sang but never recorded the songs, or even the origins of certain phrases or lines. There are countless times over the last year when I would be struck by a particular line from a blues song recorded in, say, 1950 and would think I'd found the original. Then, out of a scratchy recording by an obscure Delta slide player, would come the same line, recorded thirty years earlier.

Brian Robertson, aka King B
playing the blues somewhere on Sixth Street
Austin, Texas, 1996

LITTLE BLUES BOOK

SAM COLLINS

GETTING THE BLUES

There's some places in them records, there's somethin' sad in there that give you the blues; somethin' that reach back in your life or in some friend's life of yours, or that make you think of what have happened today and is so true, that if it didn't happen to you, you still got a strong idea—you know those things is goin' on. So this is very touchable, and that develops into the blues.

> JOHN LEE HOOKER,
> from *Conversations with the Blues*,
> by Paul Oliver

Big star fallin', mama . . . t'ain't long before day.
Maybe this sunshine will drive these blues away.

> BLIND WILLIE MCTELL
> *"Mama T'ain't Long
> Before Day"*

Sometimes I want to holler,
sometimes I want to shout.
Sometimes I want to cry,
and I wonder what about.
I think I got the blues.

> SONNY TERRY
> *"I Think I Got the Blues"*

I went downtown and bought myself a pair of shoes.
I didn't do it 'cause I needed them,
did it because I had the blues.
> LIGHTNIN' HOPKINS
> *"Go Home with Me"*

Blues before sunrise, tears standing in my eyes.
It's a miserable feeling, a feeling I do despise.
> LEROY CARR
> *"Blues Before Sunrise"*

So many ways you can get the blues . . .
> BUDDY GUY
> *"One Room Country Shack"*

I'm so blue, she's got me seeing red.
> JUNIOR WELLS
> *"So Tired"*

The basic form of the blues seems to have come from various sources, including "hollers"—short rhymed verses of one or two phrases. Another major influence was the so-called "work song" that kept members of prison road gangs and work crews working together, in productive coordination.

LEROY CARR AND SCRAPPER BLACKWELL

Add to that the African-influenced five-note pentatonic scale (as opposed to the European eight-note diatonic scale), and the basis of the blues form starts to emerge.

Some people say
the Green River blues ain't bad—
then it must not have been
them Green River blues I had.

> CHARLEY PATTON
> *"Green River Blues"*

I got off my pallet and I laid down across my bed.
And when I went to eat my breakfast,
the blues were all in my bread.

> SKIP JAMES
> *"Special Rider"*

The blues grabbed my leg this morning,
tripped me, throwed me down.
Lord, I wouldn't hate it so bad
but the news done got all over town.

> TOMMY MCCLENNAN
> *"Blues Trip Me This Morning"*

Sitting by my window looking out at the rain.
You know something struck me —
clamped on my heart like a ball and chain.

BIG MAMA THORNTON
"Ball and Chain"

People have different blues and think they're mighty sad,
but blues about a man — the worst I ever had.

MA RAINEY
(title unknown)

Blues came walking in my room. I said,
"Blues, please tell me what you are doing
to make me feel so blue?"
They looked at me and smiled, but refused to say.
I seen them again and they turned and walked away.

IDA COX
"Rambling Blues"

Got the blues so bad, I can hardly sleep at night.
Tried to eat my meal, my teeth refused to bite.

ORA BROWN
"Jinx Blues"

Soon one morning, the blues knocked on my door.
"Come here to stay with you, won't be leaving no more."

> MANCE LIPSCOMB
> *"Goin' to Louisiana"*

Out last night with wild women and it gave me the Big Night Blues.

> BLIND LEMON JEFFERSON
> *"Big Night Blues"*

You know the blues ain't nothing
but a low-down shaking, empty chill.
Well if you ain't never had 'em, honey,
I hope you never will.

> SON HOUSE
> *"The Jinx Blues"*

The word *blues* originally had nothing to do with sadness; it seems to have meant a state of mind more akin to boredom. By the early 1800s, however, the term *blue devils* came to signify contrary spirits that hung around and caused sadness. This was shortened when Washington Irving coined the phrase "the blues."

Songs that were to become known as blues did exist in some basic form before the turn of the century, but they were called

SON HOUSE

ditties by those who performed them. The first use of the word *blues* in the title of a piece of music was found in "The Dallas Blues," published in March 1912 by Hart Wand. The story goes that Wand played his violin in the back of his father's drugstore. One day a black porter heard Wand play a melody he could whistle along with and remarked, "That give me the blues to go back to Dallas." That comment provided Wand with the inspiration for the song title.

It was W. C. Handy, though, who first popularized the blues with his publication of "Memphis Blues" (1912) and "St. Louis Blues" (1914). The first recorded vocal blues song is thought to have been "Crazy Blues," released in 1920 by Mamie Smith.

I got the blues so bad,
it hurt my tongue to talk.
I would follow my baby,
but it hurt my feet to walk.
> TAMPA RED
> *"Seminole Blues"*

I was in my room and I bowed down to pray—
then the blues came along and blowed my spirit away.
> SON HOUSE
> *"Preachin' the Blues"*

Blues in my mailbox
'cause I can't get no mail,
blues in my bread-box
'cause my bread got stale.

> MERLINE JOHNSON
> (THE YAS YAS GIRL)
> *"Blues Everywhere"*

I make my living feeling rotten,
but I feel good when I play the blues.

> JOHNNY WINTER
> *"World of Contradictions"*

First time I met the blues, mama,
they came walking through the wood.
They stopped at my house first, mama,
and done me all the harm they could.

> LITTLE BROTHER
> MONTGOMERY
> *"The First Time I Met You"*

Went to the mountain and looked down in the sea—
minnows had my woman and the blues had me.

> SLEEPY JOHN ESTES
> *"Stack O'Dollars Blues"*

The blues is a worried old heart disease.

SON HOUSE
"The Jinx Blues"

He would sit all night long feeling bad and just continue singing and playing, improvising one song after another, and tears would stream from his eyes. And he'd get other people crying. Then, sometimes, he would be on another kick, you know . . . love. He'd just love women. Listening to him he'd make you think you were, well . . . this can't be written down, but you know what I mean. That is, you couldn't understand what the hell he was singing, but you didn't have to.

JOSH WHITE, on
Blind Lemon Jefferson

I'm so poor I have to lean up against a fence to gargle.

BIG BILL BROONZY
"Looking Up at Down"

I have Uneda biscuits here
and half a pint of gin.
The gin is mighty fine
but them biscuits are a little too thin.

BLIND LEMON JEFFERSON
"Rabbit Foot Blues"

BLIND LEMON JEFFERSON

It's been so dry,
you could make a powder house out of the world.

>   SON HOUSE
>   *"Dry Spell Blues"*

Please give me a match
to light this short I've found.
I know it looks bad for me,
picking tobacco up off the ground.

>   DOC CLAYTON
>   *"On the Killing Floor"*

HOW TO WRITE YOUR OWN BLUES SONG

First, feel really bad. Or really good. The point is to feel.

Second, come up with a line that expresses how you're feeling at the moment, such as:

My baby's got a heart like a rock at the bottom of the sea.

Then, simply repeat that line.

My baby's got a heart like a rock at the bottom of the sea.

So far, so good! Now, the third step is to come up with a finishing line that rhymes or comes close to rhyming with the first. In this case, how about:

My baby's built for the blues, and I guess it's too bad for me.

Now, it might be time for a title, which is often the "hook" line that forms the rhyme and repeats at the end of each verse. In this case, I've just written out one of my songs, "Built for the Blues." From a music standpoint, the blues uses the I, IV, and V chords of the key it's in. For example, suppose we write out "Built for the Blues" in the key of E. The chord pattern (using another verse) would be:

  E (I)   *E (I)*
She's got long slender fingers made to double-cross
          A (IV)   *E (I)*
She's got long slender fingers made to double-cross
        B7 (V7)   *A (IV)*   *E (I)*
My baby's built for the blues and I guess it's just my loss.

BAD LUCK AND MAD MEN

I'm tired of being worried every day.
Seems there's detour signs keeping good things away.
>> JUKE BOY BONNER
>> *"I'm Getting Tired"*

That tough luck has sunk me
and the rats is gettin' in my hat.
>> BLIND LEMON JEFFERSON
>> *"Tin Cup Blues"*

God knows, I helped that little woman
when she could not help herself,
and as soon as Juke Boy got in bad luck
she split with someone else.
>> JUKE BOY BONNER
>> *(title unknown)*

Born under a bad sign,
been down since I began to crawl.
If it wasn't for bad luck,
I wouldn't have no luck at all.
>> ALBERT KING
>> *"Born Under a Bad Sign"*

Lady Luck has never smiled on me,
I've never saw her wonderful face.
If it was raining soup,
I'd be caught with a fork.

> MERCY DEE
> *"Lady Luck"*

I want to go home and I ain't got sufficient clothes,
doggone my bad-luck soul.

> BLIND LEMON JEFFERSON
> *"Bad Luck Blues"*

Got me accused of forgery and I can't even write my name.

> TEXAS ALEXANDER
> *"Levee Camp Moan Blues"*

Talk about bad luck and the blues? Honeyboy Edwards (b. 1915) missed the commercial success granted to some other blues talents, largely because his career breaks would have given anybody the blues. When Alan Lomax toured the South and discovered Muddy Waters, he also interviewed and recorded Edwards, but technical problems ruined the tapes. Later Edwards journeyed to Memphis and recorded two songs for the Sun label, but fate struck again. The tapes were put aside for more than twenty years and, when released, were somehow credited to a piano player by the name of Albert Williams.

Edwards made it to Chicago and was actually recorded by Leonard Chess, but there was a problem with the songs selected. Muddy Waters laid claim to some of the material, and to avoid conflict, Chess shelved Edwards's versions. Edwards's career floundered again.

Then Edwards helped start up the Aces, which included Louis Myers, David Myers, Junior Wells, and Fred Below, the latter being one of the great blues drummers of all time. The band became an institution over the years, with members coming and going and staging reunions. As for Edwards, he had left the band before they made their first recording and thus missed their success.

In 1963 Honeyboy Edwards took part in a Chess session with Otis Spann, Big Walter Horton, Willie Dixon, and the British band Fleetwood Mac. Almost predictably, the engineer accidentally erased the only two tracks Edwards sang lead on.

I'm lame and blind, can't hardly see.
My doggone daddy turned his back on me.
I ain't got nobody to really comfort me.
LOTTIE KIMBROUGH
"Going Away Blues"

I twisted and I tumbled,
I rolled the whole night long.
I didn't have no daddy
to hold me in his arms.

> GEECHIE WILEY
> *"Eagles on a Half"*

Should have seen me, man, around the break of day —
huggin' on that pillow where my baby used to lay.

> SON HOUSE
> *"Death Letter Blues"*

I done seen better days,
but I'm putting up with these.

> RABBIT BROWN
> *(title unknown)*

If I was a bird I'd find a nest in the heart of town,
So when the times get lonesome I'd be bird nest bound.

> CHARLEY PATTON
> *"Bird Nest Bound"*

There were two bluesmen who called themselves
Sonny Boy Williamson — the first was John Lee Williamson

(1914–1948) and the other, an eccentric surrealist of the blues, was Aleck "Rice" Miller (1910–1965), referred to in this book as Sonny Boy Williamson II. It was the original Sonny Boy Williamson who was "ganged" and attacked by someone using an ice pick while walking from one club to another in Chicago. He was found dead with reportedly seventeen holes in his head, although the actual number of wounds was probably lower and increased with each telling, in the best blues tradition. Sonny Boy was married to a woman named Lacey Belle, who was mentioned in several of his tunes. A variation on the legend has it that she returned to her home and found her beloved Sonny Boy, who had struggled there from the streets after being attacked. Breathing his last breath in her arms, he said only: "Lord have mercy."

I didn't build this world,
but I sure can tear it down.
>   PLEASANT JOE
>   *"Sawmill Man Blues"*

Lord, she brought me coffee and she brought me tea.
Fell dead at the door with the jailhouse key.
>   SAM COLLINS
>   *"Jailhouse Blues"*

If I got thrown in the Love Prison,
not a single woman here tonight would go my bail.
>> BRIAN ROBERTSON
>> *"Grandpa's Kite"*

If I don't go crazy,
I will surely lose my mind.
>> SON HOUSE
>> *"Louise McGee"*

Look out!
I got the madman blues!
>> JOHN LEE HOOKER
>> *"Madman Blues"*

I'm so tore up and bothered,
I don't even trust myself.
>> MERCY DEE
>> *"Call the Asylum"*

Blind Willie Johnson (1900–1950) made astonishing music that is a potent mixture of blues and gospel, a stunning blend of slide guitar and fierce vocals. While many players used the slide to provide a counterpoint of rhythm or mood,

BLIND WILLIE JOHNSON

Johnson's slide echoed the delivery and tone of his vocal style. The story has come down that Johnson was blinded at a young age when his stepmother threw lye into his eyes during a fight with Johnson's father. Among his most powerful works is the famous "Motherless Children Have a Hard Time" and his stunning "God Don't Never Change." It is said that the spirited "If I Had My Way I'd Tear the Building Down" was so intense that when Johnson sang it in front of the customshouse in New Orleans, he was arrested for inciting a riot.

GOOD TIMES

I used to go around to where the old boys was—boys was playing guitars and one thing and another—and I used to go around to dances. Oh, they was good dances. Them womens be flatfoot shaking it, and them people cut up with them guitars. And I said if ever I got to be, you know, my own man, I was going to learn to play a guitar.

WILLIAM DIAMOND,
from *Blow My Blues Away*,
by George Mitchell

Won't be worried with these blues no more—
said it's train time now,
hear that ring I do adore.

BAREFOOT BILL
"Squabbling Blues"

Let your hair down, baby.
Let's have a natural ball.
If you don't let you hair down baby,
we can't have no fun at all.

T-BONE WALKER
"T-Bone Shuffle"

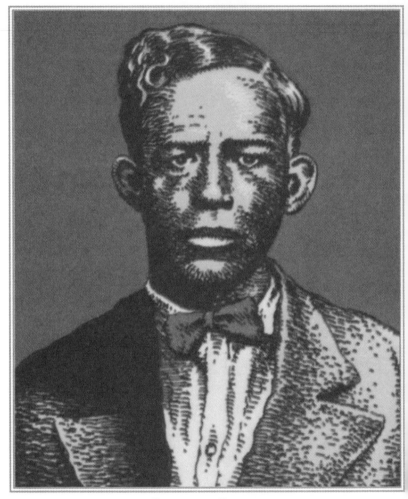

CHARLEY PATTON

We gonna pitch our wang dang doodle all night long.
>   WILLIE DIXON
>   *"Wang Dang Doodle"*

I'm a crazy mixed up kid
and I love to dance like this.
In case you haven't heard,
this is a crazy mixed up world.
>   LITTLE WALTER
>   *"Crazy Mixed Up World"*

Charley Patton (1891–1934) is regarded as the first famous Delta bluesman. Certainly, he was one of the first to record. With Patton, the line between legend and fact blurs. He was said to have been married eight times and is remembered as being prone to violence, heavy drinking, and smoking. Yet the one faded photograph of Patton that exists reveals none of that. A bow tie tilted slightly too much to one side, a bit of a bewildered look, oversized ears, the suggestion of a racially mixed heritage—all of this doesn't explain the man who, it is said, would play his guitar over his head or behind his back or—shades of Chuck Berry and Jimi Hendrix—between his legs. No matter what the truth about Patton, his voice lives on in those he influenced—most notably Son

House, Robert Johnson, Howlin' Wolf, John Lee Hooker, and Elmore James.

Although apparently Patton died in bed from an infection, the popular tales of his demise were quite a bit more in the bluesman mold. The common belief was that he was killed by a woman armed with a razor, a story that was perhaps grounded in the fact that Patton's throat was slashed during a barroom fight, after which he recovered and continued to record in a slightly raspy voice. Still, myths have their way of spreading, and bluesman Bukka White once said that although he'd like to have been a Charley Patton, he didn't like the thought that "one of them old sandfoot womens" might walk up and "cut my throat or do something that's unnecessary."

S ay you little girl with the black dress on—
come over here, stand by me.
Let me show you how to do the Head Rag Hop.
ROMEO NELSON
"Head Rag Hop"

D ance with me baby,
but don't move around so fast.
B. B. KING
"Dance with Me Baby"

Wake up every morning
with a jinx all around my bed.
I have been a good provider,
but I believe I been mislead.
CHARLEY PATTON
"Revenue Man Blues"

I can't have good times like I used to have had.
My regular found out I'm a Saturday night spender
and it sure did make her mad.
BLIND LEMON JEFFERSON
"Saturday Night Spender Blues"

When Muddy Waters (1915–1983) recorded "Can't Be Satisfied," Leonard Chess of the legendary Chess record label felt he had a loser on his hands. He listened to the record and shook his head, saying, "I can't understand what he's singing!" The record was distributed to a variety of outlets on the South Side of Chicago, including beauty salons and barbershops. Within a few hours, there wasn't a copy to be found. As for Muddy, who was working as a driver delivering venetian blinds, he had to pay for a copy—only to be charged $1.10 for a 79¢ record and be told that the record was being strictly rationed—one per customer!

I know my little baby,
she gonna jump and shout
when that train be late, boys,
and I come walking out.

MUDDY WATERS
"Can't Be Satisfied"

Mama told papa, "Let that child boogie.
It's in him, and it's gotta come out."

JOHN LEE HOOKER
"Boogie Chill'in"

I got a woman take care of me.
Yes, she's just only sweet sixteen.
I never done a day's work in my life.
I don't even know what work means.

PEETIE WHEATSTRAW
"Confidence Man"

We lived in the country and they gave a party one night. I went over there and played for them that night and got drunk. I had never got drunk before. I was playing the blues and I came home the next morning singing the blues. My dad said, 'Boy, get out of here, you've been drinking that rotgut whiskey.' I wasn't but fourteen.

> HONEYBOY EDWARDS,
> from an interview with
> David S. Rotenstein

I'd rather be sloppy drunk
than anything I know.
Another half a pint, woman,
you'll see me go.

> SONNY BOY WILLIAMSON
> *"Sloppy Drunk"*

I don't care what people are thinking.
I ain't drunk, I'm just drinking.

> ALBERT COLLINS
> *"I Ain't Drunk"*

I got the world in a jug
and the stopper in my hand.

> ALBERTA HUNTER
> *"Down Hearted Blues"*

Whiskey straight will drive the blues away.
That be the case, I want a quart today.

MISSISSIPPI JOHN HURT
"Got the Blues"

Hound Dog Taylor (1917–1975) was one of the greats of wild party blues. His own life was shortened by his alcohol intake, which was, it is said, quite astonishing. At one point, Brewer Phillips, Hound Dog's second guitar player, discovered that the mixture of Hound Dog and alcohol meant something evil was going on.

Hound Dog got up from the couch and he went like he was going to the bathroom, which I wasn't paying him no attention. I was sitting on the couch. Hound Dog came back with a rifle and said, "Hey, Brewer." And pointed the rifle—pow! Shot me right through the side. I said, "Hound Dog. What did you shoot me for?" And he shot me through this finger and then he shot me through the shoulder. If that rifle hadn't jammed, he probably would have hurt me.

BREWER PHILLIPS,
interview with John Anthony Brisbin,
Living Blues

I did more for you baby,
than the good Lord ever done—
I put hair on your head
and you know he didn't give you none.

> HOUND DOG TAYLOR
> *"Give Me Back That Wig"*

Bring me my pistol, shotgun, and some shells.
I've been mistreated baby,
now I'm gonna raise some hell.

> PEETIE WHEATSTRAW
> *"Ain't It a Pity and a Shame"*

Now you know you didn't want me
when you lay down 'cross my bed,
drinking your moonshine whiskey,
talking all out of your head.

> BLIND BOY FULLER
> *"Pistol Slapper Blues"*

When I ain't got no liquor,
look like everything I do go wrong.
That's when I get evil,
me and the devil can't get along.

> CLARE MORRIS
> *"I Staggered in My Sleep"*

PEETIE WHEATSTRAW

Moonshine will make you go home,
lay down across your bed.
And your wife try to talk to you,
you say you didn't hear a word she said.

> SONNY BOY WILLIAMSON
> *"Moonshine"*

It takes boozy booze, Lord,
to carry me through.

> CHARLEY PATTON
> *"High Sheriff Blues"*

You know I'm black and I'm evil,
but I did not make myself.

> LIGHTNIN' HOPKINS
> *"Black and Evil"*

Peetie Wheatstraw (1902–1941) is one of the more unique characters in blues. He nicknamed himself the High Sheriff of Hell and did everything he could to play off the role of the darkness in blues, even declaring himself the Devil's Son-in-Law on one of his records. At the same time, his attitude toward things was much lighter than Robert Johnson's, and one gets the sense that if there's a hell in Wheatstraw's music, it is simply that he was having one hell of a good time.

CLIFFORD GIBSON

Baby fix me one more drink
and hug your daddy one more time.
Keep on stirring my malted milk
till I change my mind.

ROBERT JOHNSON
"Malted Milk Blues"

Get my lips to a bottle every once in awhile.
Now everything's crazy. I got one big smile.
But the question I'm asking is, "Where did my legs go?"

JOHN MAYALL
"Where Did My Legs Go?"

I'm crazy about my whiskey,
I love my good gin.
Every time I take a drink
I go floating in the wind.

BROWNIE AND SONNY
"Feel So Good"

What's that, baby, pecking on your windowpane?
(The stars is shining so I know it can't be rain.)

CLIFFORD GIBSON
"Keep Your Windows Pinned"

I'm so glad good whiskey made it through.
It have saved my wife from dying
and saved my sweetheart, too.

PEETIE WHEATSTRAW
"More Good Whiskey Blues"

Mississippi John Hurt (1893–1966) was one of the most beloved blues artists of all time. After recording in 1928 for Okeh records, he vanished from sight. At age seventy-one, Hurt was rediscovered in Mississippi and subsequently spent the last few years of his life playing at coffeehouses and festivals. Folklorist Tom Hoskins had been able to find Hurt through some careful detective work—including letting the music tell him where to look. Hurt's 1928 recording of "Avalon Blues" mentioned "Avalon, my home town," and this led Hoskins to the bluesman, who was clearly astonished to know anyone even remembered him. For the six 78s released from those first sessions, Hurt had been paid twenty dollars a song.

His stick of candy don't melt away,
just gets better so the ladies say.

MISSISSIPPI JOHN HURT
"Candy Man"

MISSISSIPPI JOHN HURT

SOMETIMES YOU'RE LONESOME

Don't the sun look lonesome
setting down behind the trees?
Don't your house look lonesome
when your baby's packed to leave?

> MUDDY WATERS
> *"Blow Wind Blow"*

I would go out and sit under the old oak tree,
but I ain't got nobody to talk baby talk to me.

> THE HONEY DRIPPER
> *"The Train Is Coming"*

Don't your house look lonesome
when your dough-roller gone?
'Cause it gonna kill you,
cooking till she comes home.

> MISSISSIPPI FRED MCDOWELL
> *"Gravel Road Blues"*

You talk about lonely—
do you know what loneliness is all about?

> J. C. BURRIS
> *"Loneliness"*

Lonesome, baby, when you're out of sight.
God up in heaven know you ain't doing me right.
> LIGHTNIN' HOPKINS
> *"Lonesome Lightnin'"*

She's been gone twenty-four hours
and that's twenty-three hours too long.
> JAMES COTTON
> *"23 Hours Too Long"*

Tell me baby, what's the matter now?
You tried to quit me but you don't know how?
> BARBECUE BOB &
> LAUGHING CHARLIE
> *"It Won't Be Long Now"*

The diddley bow, from which Bo Diddley (b. 1928) took his name, was an instrument made from a single strand of baling wire or broom straw stretched tight along a barn or piece of wood, with a rock as a crude bridge. Music was made by either hitting at it with the fingers or using the neck off a glass bottle, crafted into what became known as a slide. The bottleneck guitar in blues was the next step after the diddley bow, and seems to have been influenced by slack key guitar, a Hawaiian style popular before World War I. Unlike notes on the classical guitar or piano, pitches played with a slide are less fixed. The movement between notes, the rubato timing, the open tuning, and the mixture of scales combine to create a powerful sound that mimics the human voice — and invokes the voice of the blues.

Ain't it hard to love a woman
when that woman don't love you?
You know she have your poor mind on wanderin'
and you don't know what in the world you want to do.

> LIGHTNIN' HOPKINS
> *"Hard to Love a Woman"*

How long you gonna do me wrong?
Ain't nobody ever lived
that didn't do somebody wrong, wrong, wrong.

> HOWLIN' WOLF
> *"Baby How Long"*

When I kiss you,
why did you tremble so?
I realize this is your first affair,
but I just can't let you go.

> OLLIE SHEPARD
> *"Little Pigmeat"*

I walk forty-seven miles of barbed wire,
got a cobra snake for a necktie,
a house down by the roadside,
made out of rattlesnake hide.
Cut me a chimney in the very top
and it's made out of human skull.
Come on, take a little walk with me and tell me—
who do you love?

BO DIDDLEY
"Who Do You Love?"

I'm a man.

BO DIDDLEY
"I'm a Man"

If you didn't want me, woman,
why did you dog me around?

SONNY TERRY
"Burnt Child"

BLUES ON THE ROAD

Standing down at the crossroads, a young musician strums his guitar and waits for a tap on the shoulder. When that cold touch is felt, the musician hands over the guitar (without looking), and the Devil takes it and plays a couple of tunes. When the devil hands it back, the musician has the ability to play whatever he wants.

But at a price.

This tale is at the center of the legend of Robert Johnson (1912–1938), the archetypal bluesman/drifter. Apparently able to play a wide variety of music that ranged from popular tunes to, as some said, anything he'd heard played one time, Robert Johnson is best known for his blues, which include "Crossroads," "Ramblin' on My Mind," and "Terraplane Blues." Johnson would show up to play in juke joints where musicians such as Son House would only reluctantly allow him to come on stage because Johnson's guitar playing was about the worst they'd ever seen. Johnson disappeared for about a year and then showed up again, boldly asking if he could take the stage. He did and, by all accounts, launched into a powerful display of emotional pyrotechnics that left everyone amazed. From this—and from Johnson himself—came the story of the crossroads.

Johnson's death is attributed to poisoning. The reason for the killing? Johnson's habit of picking out a woman in the audience—single or married—and bit by bit directing each song in her direction, working his slow seduction. It's said that on one particular night, Johnson's magic worked so well that a woman's husband—the bartender—retaliated by giving the bluesman a bottle of whiskey laced with poison.

Whatever the case, Johnson's life and legend have come to be seen as a personification of the blues—the undercurrents of evil, the mystery, the lightheartedness, the sexual heat and energy, the joy and the life on the road where one moves constantly to avoid the hellhounds on the trail.

I got ramblin' on my mind.
Hates to leave my baby,
but she treats me so unkind.

>ROBERT JOHNSON
>*"Ramblin' on My Mind"*

She is the little Queen of Spades,
and men will not leave her alone.
Every time she makes a spread,
cold chills just run all over me.

>ROBERT JOHNSON
>*"Little Queen of Spades"*

Woke up this morning,
looked around for my shoes.
You could tell by that
I had them mean old walking blues.

ROBERT JOHNSON
"Walking Blues"

Stones in my passageway
and my road seems dark at night.

ROBERT JOHNSON
"Stones in My Passway"

I'm a stranger here,
just blowed in your town.
If I ask for a favor,
please don't turn me down.

WILLIE BAKER
"No No Blues"

Don't ever drive a stranger from your door.
It might be your best friend.
It might be your brother,
you will never know.

LONNIE JOHNSON
"Careless Love"

You know there ain't nothin' in ramblin'.
>> MEMPHIS MINNIE
>> *"Nothing in Ramblin'"*

Drifting and drifting, just like a ship out on the sea.
I ain't got nobody in this world to care for me.
>> JOHN LEE HOOKER
>> *"Drifter Blues"*

I'm a stranger here,
just came in on the train.
Won't some good man tell me
some woman's name?
>> BLIND LEMON JEFFERSON
>> *"Stocking Feet Blues"*

Crying, ain't going down this big road by myself.
If I don't carry you, girl, gonna carry somebody else.
>> TOMMY JOHNSON
>> *"Big Road Blues"*

I have worn out my shoes
and now I'm wearing out my socks.
>> MUDDY WATERS
>> *"No Escape from the Blues"*

If you don't believe I'm leaving,
just watch the train I'm on.
If you don't believe I'm leaving,
just count the days I'm gone.

ISHMAN BRACEY
"Leaving Town Blues"

The blues grabbed mama's child and tore it upside down.

ROBERT JOHNSON
"Preaching Blues"

Leonard and Paul Chess were the owners of Chess Records, and their roster of artists reads like a *Who's Who* of Chicago blues: Muddy Waters, Howlin' Wolf, Willie Dixon, Little Walter, Elmore James, Sonny Boy Williamson II (Rice Miller), Buddy Guy, Bo Diddley, Jimmy Rogers, and many, many more. Originally from Poland, the Chez family arrived in America in 1928 and soon changed their name, Americanizing it to *Chess.* From a start in the liquor business, the brothers graduated to a group of stores and some clubs. It was at one of their establishments, the Macomba Club, that some of blues greats mentioned above got their start. The brothers noticed that the major labels were ignoring the new up-and-coming blues sound in favor of the older, more sedate versions. Believing in the new style's possibility for success, in 1947 the brothers entered the recording business.

One of the most famous exchanges ever recorded on tape at Chess wasn't music at all, but rather a rolling, cursing argument that involved Leonard Chess and Sonny Boy Williamson II, which is now finally available on CD. The two have a heated discussion over the title of one of Williamson's more surrealistic songs, "Little Village." "Call it your mammy if you want," Sonny Boy shouts in one rather tame moment. Elsewhere in the same discussion, the rather eccentric bluesman shouts another, less flattering term involving the word *mother* at Chess.

Ramblin' round with this woman
caused me to be down so low,
and now my dear old mother
won't allow me round her door.
> LEROY CARTER
> *"Cruel Woman Blues"*

Nobody loves me but my mother,
and she may be jivin', too.
> B. B. KING
> *"Nobody Loves Me
> but My Mother"*

I'm a stranger in this place
and I'm looking for my mama's grave.

> BUKKA WHITE
> *"Strange Place"*

I'm gonna leave here walking,
make home my second stop.
I'm gonna find my mother,
she's the only friend I got.

> SONNY JONES
> *"Won't Somebody Pacify
> My Mind"*

Write my mother,
tell her the shape I'm in.
Tell her to pray for me,
forgiveness for my sins.

> MANCE LIPSCOMB
> *"Goin' Down Slow"*

It's a long way from the blues clubs of Beale Street in Memphis to being honored by the U.S. Senate with the title Ambassador-at-Large of Good Will and by the French government as a Commander of Arts and Letters. But Memphis Slim

(1915–1988) made that trip in style. A fine blues pianist, Memphis Slim wrote one of the great anthems of the blues, "Everyday I Have the Blues," along with his trademark, "Beer Drinking Woman." While touring Europe in 1960, Memphis Slim found the adulation and support irresistible. He relocated to Paris in 1962.

I got the railroad blues,
got boxcars on my mind.

JAMES YANK RACHEL
"T-Bone Steak Blues"

I had so much trouble,
swear my nerves is weakenin' down.
I would swing on a freight train,
but I'm afraid to leave the ground.

BUMBLE BEE SLIM
"If I Make It Over"

When it all comes down,
you got to go back to Mother Earth.

MEMPHIS SLIM
"Mother Earth"

I'm a brokenhearted bachelor,
traveling through this wide world alone.
It's the railroad for my pillow,
this jungle for my happy home.

SON BONDS
"Old Bachelor Blues"

Something tells me I won't be here long —
I got my suitcase packed
and my trunk's already gone.

L. C. WILLIAMS
"I Won't Be Here Long"

Memphis Minnie (1897–1973), known as the Hoodoo
Lady, managed to create a legendary presence in the world of
the blues, largely a man's club. Big Bill Broonzy (whom she
reportedly beat in a blues contest in Chicago in the 1930s) said,
"She plays guitar like a man!" Indeed, there are a number of
legends about her, including accounts of her playing electric
guitar before 1942 and wearing two bracelets fashioned from
silver dollars. At the end of her life, the attention of a few
singers, journalists, and researchers saved her from feeling
that she had been completely forgotten.

MEMPHIS MINNIE

Ain't nothing in rambling,
either running round.
I believe I'll marry, Lord,
and settle down.

MEMPHIS MINNIE
"Nothing in Rambling"

Going back to my used to be,
although she has done me wrong.
Well, I think I'll forgive her,
'cause I'm tired of drifting through this world alone.

WILLIE BROWN
"Mississippi Blues"

The highway is like a woman—
soft shoulders and dangerous curves.

ALBERT COLLINS
"Highway"

Been down so many highways,
I can see them all in my dreams.

CHARLIE MUSSLEWHITE
"Highway Blues"

I'm going to leave you,
but I'll be back some old day.
I'm gonna make you remember
how you drove me away.

FUNNY PAPA SMITH
"Dreaming Blues"

Sitting here wondering
would a matchbox hold my clothes?
I don't want to be bothered
with no suitcase on the road.

LEADBELLY
"Packin' Trunk Blues"

I got the key to the highway,
so now I'm bound to go.
I'm gonna leave here runnin'
cause walkin's much too slow.

BROWNIE AND SONNY
"Key to the Highway"

It's a good time here, but it's better down the road.

LIGHTNIN' HOPKINS
"Better Down the Road"

MEMPHIS JUG BAND

I can sit here, think a thousand miles away.
MEMPHIS JUG BAND
"Beale Street Mess Around"

BIG CITY BLUES

Although some people assume the blues spread from the rural areas into the big cities, it's more accurate to say it moved from south to north. Indeed, the earliest blues songs were performed in large Southern cities such as New Orleans. Little by little, the blues began to move north, toward towns such as Chicago. Those who relocated from the South brought with them an appreciation for a culture and a music that served to bind together an entire community of people.

Here I am in the big city
and I'm just about to starve to death.
My sister that lives in the country
got cattle, hogs, and chickens layin' in the nest.
    JUKE BOY BONNER
    "Big City Blues"

Women folk go around flaggin' the menfolk down.
And I ain't jivin' when I say Houston's the action town.
    JUKE BOY BONNER
    "Houston's the Action Town"

If a man can make it in Los Angeles,
he can make it anywhere.
But you got to have one of those Cadillac cars.
CHARLES WATERFORD
"L.A. Blues"

Lightnin' Hopkins (1912–1982) was one of the true giants of the blues, a unique character who was apt to pull lyrics out of the air at any moment and who would record with anyone who paid—up front. In spite of that, his collection of work is astonishingly powerful, fun, and telling. Few performers in any area have let as much of their lives, thoughts, and feelings be put on tape, so much so that the work becomes an autobiography, a testimony to one man's life. That life included a public performance at age eight with the legendary Blind Lemon Jefferson at a country picnic, time in Big Brazos Penitentiary, and travel around the world thanks to his "discovery" during the folk music period of the 1960s.

His nickname came from an early career association with Wilson Smith, a pianist nicknamed Thunder. Aladdin Records paired them up, and the duo became known as Lightnin' and Thunder.

You better move your baby —
I might tell her to go home with me.

> LIGHTNIN' HOPKINS
> *"Got to Move Your Baby"*

Baby, I can't drink whiskey
but I'm a fool about my homemade wine.
Ain't no sense in leaving Dallas,
they make it there all the time.

> BLIND LEMON JEFFERSON
> *"Chock House Blues"*

There's some streets in Houston
I stay clear of after dark,
'cause there's some cat that'll bump you off
just to hear his pistol bark.

> JUKE BOY BONNER
> *"Struggle Here in Houston"*

Say, I ain't going down to third alley
unless I change my mind.
'Cause you know I done got shot over there, Lord,
and stabbed three or four times.

> WALTER ROLAND
> *"45 Pistol Blues"*

I can't see what brought me here.
Must have been this new canned city beer.
>LOTTIE KIMBROUGH
>*"Going Away Blues"*

Did you ever see a one-eyed woman cry?
>LIGHTNIN' HOPKINS
>*(title unknown)*

Bright lights, big city went to my baby's head.
>VARIOUS ARTISTS
>*"Bright Lights, Big City"*

EVIL-HEARTED WOMAN

The great Louisiana swamp blues found on Excello Records contain some of the most amazing blues sounds ever captured. Jay Miller was the spirit behind Excello, and he had rather creative ways of getting the best out of his artists. Of course, this is the same Jay Miller who listened to Slim Harpo (1924–1970; author of "King Bee," "Scratch My Back," and other classics) and said Harpo sounded "like a whole lot of guys who don't sell a whole lot of records."

Perhaps the one example that best illustrates Miller's methods is the story that he paid Lightnin' Slim's girlfriend (or wife, depending upon who you ask) twenty-five dollars to make Lightnin' Slim's life a living hell for three days before the bluesman went in for a recording session. If a really special tune came out of the deal, the woman received a bonus in the form of a pretty new dress. In many blues songs, one gets the feeling that making life difficult for one's lover is something that happens on a regular basis for a lot less than twenty-five dollars.

Devil got ninety thousand women —
he just need one more.

KING SOLOMON HILL
"Whoopee Blues"

Sometimes I think, ma,
you're too sweet to die.
Then again, I think
you ought to be buried alive.

FUNNY PAPA SMITH
"Dreaming Blues"

Just want to see my old gal again
when she ain't got so evil,
she ain't got too many men.

SONNY BOY WATSON
"Rumble Go the Train"

You a no-good woman,
don't mean no man no good.
If I didn't love you,
I would not if I could.

TOMMIE BRADLEY
"Window Pane Blues"

I was burned once, in 1944,
but woman I ain't gonna let that happen no more.
I'm a burnt child, and I'm afraid of fire.

SONNY TERRY
"Burnt Child"

I got the meanest woman you ever seen—
she sleeps with an ice pick in her hand
and she fights all in her dreams.
I been dealing with the devil.

> SONNY BOY WILLIAMSON
> *"Dealing with the Devil"*

Take a mighty crooked woman
to treat a good man wrong.

> WILLIE BAKER
> *"No No Blues"*

My baby thinks she's a black panther,
she wants to climb up in the tree and jump down.
She wants to cut my throat
when there ain't nobody else around.

> SONNY BOY WILLIAMSON
> *"Black Panther Blues"*

She's an evil-hearted woman.
She studies evil all the time.

> ROBERT JOHNSON
> *"Kindhearted Woman Blues"*

SKIP JAMES

I'd rather be the devil than that old woman's man.
> KANSAS JOE MCCOY
> *(title unknown)*

Nothing but the devil change my baby's mind.
> SKIP JAMES
> *"Devil Got My Woman"*

You work all day on your job,
you come home your woman is gone.
There's a note somewhere on the table saying
"fix your own meals" and she'll be home.
Boys, it's time for a change.
> JUKE BOY BONNER
> *"Time to Make a Change"*

THE BLUES SOUNDS LIKE
AN EMPTY POCKET

You can't be a good musician and field hand at the same time. You got to be one or the other, and if you are a musician, the white man taught the black man he was no good. Keep him away from your house because he's after your wife. He's after your daughter. You understand what I mean? And some of it was true, see, I mean, just because he's a musician, I don't say that he's thorough . . . he's cleansed, he's holy. You got some dirty people in all walks of life. Look at the politicians and people like that. Look at the things they have to cover up and sweep under the rug, and why in the hell should a musician be any better?

> JOHNNY SHINES,
> in *Sounds Good to Me*,
> by Barry Lee Pearson

I'm gonna get me a picket
off a graveyard fence,
gonna beat you brownskin
till you learn some good sense.

> STOVEPIPE NUMBER 1
> *"Court Street Blues"*

Next time the bossman hit me,
I'm gonna give him a big surprise.

LIGHTNIN' HOPKINS
"Penitentiary Blues"

Captain got a big horse pistol
and he thinks he's bad.
I'm gonna take it this mornin'
if he makes me mad.

BESSIE TUCKER
"Key to the Bushes"

Big boss man,
can't you hear me when I call?
You ain't so big.
You just tall, that's all.

JIMMY REED
"Big Boss Man"

I asked my captain for the time of day.
He said he throwed his watch away.

CHARLIE LINCOLN
"Chain Gang Trouble"

Now work was made for two things—
that was a fool and a mule.

PEETIE WHEATSTRAW
"Confidence Man"

WORKING BLUES

In tough times, bluesmen took on a variety of jobs to allow them to play their music.

Bobby Blue Bland	Chauffeur/valet for B. B. King
Big Bill Broonzy	Itinerant preacher, cook, piano mover
Charles Brown	Elevator operator
Champion Jack Dupree	Boxer
Jesse "Lone Cat" Fuller	Laborer on Hollywood movie lots
John Lee Hooker	Steel mill worker
Lil' Son Jackson	Mechanic

Skip James	Minister
B. B. King	Tractor driver
Albert King	Service station attendant
Furry Lewis	Sanitation worker
Mississippi Fred McDowell	Farmworker
Jimmy Reed	Farmworker
Big Joe Turner	Bartender, bouncer, cook
Muddy Waters	Driver of a venetian blind delivery truck
Bukka White	Baseball player, boxer
Howlin' Wolf	Farmer

My body feels so wary
cause I got the miss-meal cramps.
Right now I could eat more
than a whole carload of tramps.

ALEX JOHNSON
"Miss-Meal Cramp Blues"

I heard the voice of a pork chop sing.

> JIM JACKSON
> *"Heard the Voice
> of a Pork Chop Sing"*

I been walking all day
and all night, too,
cause my meal ticket have quit me
and I can't find no work to do.

> RAMBLIN' WILLARD THOMAS
> *"No Job Blues"*

You know I haven't seen or heard of my woman
since the last day I got paid.
She said if you ain't got no money,
I ain't gonna hang around and be your maid.

> MUDDY WATERS
> *"No Escape from the Blues"*

Bukka White (1909–1977), a singer and slide guitar player, was one of the Delta bluesmen who benefited from the great rush to rediscover the blues in the 1960s. In the 1930s, White had worked under the name Washington White. He had also played baseball in the Negro leagues and had a rather brief career as a boxer. At the time he recorded two of his songs for Vocalion in Chicago, he was on the run—he'd allegedly shot a man and jumped bail after being sentenced to prison. Once captured, he ended up at the infamous Parchman Farm in Mississippi, where his music was recorded by Alan Lomax for the Library of Congress. Upon his release in the 1940s, White disappeared from public view. He was rediscovered in 1963 by John Fahey and Ed Dawson, two college students at the University of California at Berkeley, and began performing at colleges and festivals. His slashing bottleneck guitar and spirited vocals on such classic songs as "Fixin' to Die Blues" make his music powerful.

Say, if I never get a dollar
to pay this debt I owe,
I never will in this world
get in debt no more.

> TEXAS ALEXANDER
> *"Thirty Day Blues"*

She's got an old job
making four dollars a day.
I didn't have to do nothing
but lay around and throw it away.

> BILL WILBER
> *"My Babe, My Babe"*

I got a rich man's woman,
but she's living on a poor man's pay.
MUDDY WATERS
"Rich Man's Woman"

B aby, don't sic your dogs on me.
BUKKA WHITE
"Sic 'em Dogs On"

S eems like the upper-class people don't care
how the lower class of people lives.
JUKE BOY BONNER
"Don't Take Too Much"

A ll I want my babe to do
is make five dollars and give me two.
MANCE LIPSCOMB
"Sugar Babe"

O ne day I'll have money,
I want everybody to watch and see.
It's hard to keep down
a real good man like me.
SONNY BOY WILLIAMSON
"Collector Man"

I'm crazy about you baby,
but I just can't pay the price.

> EDDIE "CLEANHEAD" VINSON
> *"Kidney Stew"*

I went to this pawnshop downtown and the man had a harmonica priced at two dollars. I got a job on a soda truck, played hooky from school, worked all week, and on Saturday the man gave me a dollar and a half. For a whole week of work. I went to the pawnshop and the man said the price was two dollars. I told him I had to have the harp. He walked away from the counter, left the harp there. So, I laid my dollar and a half on the counter and picked up the harp. When the trial came up, the judge asked me why I did it. I told him I had to have the harp. The judge asked me to play it and when I did, he gave the man fifty cents and hollered, "Case dismissed."

> JUNIOR WELLS,
> in the liner notes
> to *Hoodoo Man Blues*

I'd put my guitar on my back, get to the tractor, and go down to the field. I'd plow about maybe two acres, then I'd just cut the tractor off and sit and play [laughs]. So this guy caught me playing the guitar behind the wheel. And he was mad because I didn't plow but two acres, he took my guitar and broke it across the

*tractor. I got so mad I hit him upside the head, but that didn't do
no good—he was bigger than I was. I was only fourteen years
old. So I wasn't going to work no more until I got me another
guitar. Later my mother told this guy, "What did you do that for?"
He said, "He should have been working." My mother was sancti-
fied, you know, really religious. And that was the first time I ever
heard her start to cuss. So then this guy went and bought me a
twenty-dollar guitar, but I had to promise that I wouldn't play it
on my job. I still got the guitar, the strings are way up on it now.
You can't even play it—I just look at it.*

HUBERT SUMLIN,
in *Blues Guitar*

People raving about hard times,
I don't know why they should.
If some people was like me,
they didn't have no money when times was good.

LONNIE JOHNSON
"Hard Times Ain't Gone Nowhere"

I am the king and you is the queen—
let's put our heads together,
then we can make our money green.

ROBERT JOHNSON
"Little Queen of Spades"

I remember when we first met
one Friday in the afternoon.
You said if I wanted your love, darling,
I'd have to wring the silver out of the moon.

JOHNNY SHINES
"Brutal Hearted Woman"

Here we stand, toe to toe.
I'm gonna give you this money,
ain't gonna give you no more.
She's a money taking woman.

JOHNNY YOUNG
"Money Taking Woman"

Every dollar and dime she spends
has a drop of my blood on it.

JOHNNY RUSHING
"Tricks Ain't Walking"

At big parties
I throw my money on the floor
and leave it for the sweeper,
and walk out the door.

PEETIE WHEATSTRAW
"Mr. Livingood"

Blind Boy Fuller (1907–1941) was one of the most versatile bluesmen around, recording in a variety of styles between 1935 and 1940. Born Fulton Allen, he was the quintessential street performer, known to leave recording sessions in New York City to go out on the corner and play his music for spare change. His final session was a chilling indication of his closeness to death—he sang, "My left side jumps and my flesh begin to crawl." Shortly after that session Fuller died, and in a publicity ploy that attempted to capitalize on the bluesman's popularity, the record company immediately produced another musician and billed him as Blind Boy Fuller #2. Interestingly enough, this turned out to be none other than Brownie McGhee (1915–1996), a blues figure who later became known as half of the famous blues duo Brownie and Sonny.

You're a good little girl,
but you're so stingy with me.

BLIND BOY FULLER
"Mojo Hiding Woman"

If you lose your money,
please don't lose your mind.

BROWNIE McGHEE
"If You Lose Your Money"

Bluesman Arthur "Big Boy" Crudup (1905–1974) is probably best known for his song "That's All Right," as recorded by Elvis Presley under the title "That's All Right, Mama." No matter, because Crudup never quite knew who Presley was, referring to him with mangled versions of his name such as Alvin Pretzel. A story has been widely circulated that Crudup was never paid for the song beyond a bottle of whiskey and a woman. Further, it is also said that a record company executive was ready to pay Crudup $10,000 after the fact for the song until he saw Crudup's poor state of health and said, "Hell, why bother? He'll be dead soon anyway!"

I'm through with gambling.
Some other hustler can have my room.
Well, drinking may kill me,
but gambling won't be my doom.
> LIL' SON JACKSON
> *"Gambling Blues"*

I love to gamble, gamblin's all I do,
and when I lose it never makes me blue.
I won a woman in a poker game. I lost her, too,
win another just the same.
> RED NELSON
> *"Gambling Man"*

When you lose your money,
learn to lose.

FURRY LEWIS
"Billy Lyons and Stack O'Lee"

You know I once was a gambler, boys,
but I bet my money wrong.
Now I ain't got no money and all I got is gone.

LIGHTNIN' HOPKINS
"Gambler Blues"

John Lee Hooker (b. 1917) probably recorded more albums in his time than any other bluesman. For that reason, many people have come to think of him as one of the original Delta singers, but his first recording was made in 1948. Hooker immediately carved out a unique niche in blues history as a performer—vocals that are pure deep blues and a droning guitar that is endlessly hypnotic. For Hooker, there seem to be two different kinds of songs—either slow, brooding works that hang on one chord and drill deep into a person's soul or fast boogies that hit, as Omar of the band Omar and Howlers said of good blues, "the monkey nerve."

While some of Hooker's later work is watered down by guest stars from the rock world, those cuts that consist of Hooker alone in the studio with guitar, microphone, and ever-present foot tapping are the stripped-down essence of the blues.

FOOLS FOR LOVE

If you don't believe I love you,
look what a fool I've been.
>   TEXAS ALEXANDER
>   *"98 Degree Blues"*

The night time is the right time
to be with the one you love.
Ain't no sense when night comes
and your love's so far away.
>   JOHN LEE HOOKER
>   *"In the Mood"*

Some folks are so deceiving,
take friendship as a joke.
They'll whip you when you're up
and you can't find them when you're broke.
>   TINY MAYBERRY
>   *"Mailman Blues"*

I don't mind no men friends,
but I'm scared they might cramp my style.
>   BLIND LEMON JEFFERSON
>   *"Saturday Night Spender Blues"*

When a woman gets in trouble,
everybody throws her down.
Looking for her good friend,
can't none be found.

ROBERT JOHNSON
"Come On in My Kitchen"

Can't help but worry
how my good friend done—
spent my money by the dollar,
now won't give me nickel one.

BUMBLE BEE SLIM
"No Woman, No Nickel"

Your friends think I'm a devil
and you are an innocent child.
But baby, I know different. I know you ain't.

SLIM HARPO
(title unknown)

MEN ARE FROM LOUISIANA,
WOMEN ARE FROM GEORGIA

Lucille Bogan (1897–1948?) was a blues artist who was quite at home with a single entendre. Her music contained overt reverences to lesbianism ("Women Don't Need No Men" and "B. D. [Bull Dyke] Woman's Blues"), adultery, prostitution, dope, drinking, and physical abuse. Although a rather clean version of a song called "Shave 'Em Dry" was released in 1935 by the American Record Company, a radically more risque version found its way to vinyl some years after her death. Reference books differ as to her fate. Some say she lived until 1948. Others state that she was struck and killed by an automobile upon moving to Los Angeles in or around 1935. A few tales report that she and her piano player Walter Roland simply vanished around that time. Whatever the truth, her blunt lyrical observations regarding her love of and questions about men helped to further the "tough woman" image of female blues singers that had begun as early as the 1920s.

I got nineteen men and I want one more.
If I get that one more, I'll let that nineteen go.
> BESSIE SMITH
> *"Sorrowful Blues"*

Now look here man,
what do you want me to do?
Give you my stew meat
and credit you, too?

LUCILLE BOGAN
"Stew Meat Blues"

Some are like jelly beans,
so cute and sweet.
I carry carbolic acid
for every one of them I meet.

CLARA SMITH
"Jelly Bean Blues"

Kiss me dear till I feel the string,
make me want to shake that thing.
Give me everything and how—
if you are man, then show it now.

MARY DIXON
"Papa, You Got Everything"

My handy man ain't handy no more.

ETHEL WATERS
"My Handy Man"

I ain't never loved but three men in my life.
One's my father, and my brother,
and the man that wrecked my life.

ALBERTA HUNTER
"Down Hearted Blues"

Bessie Smith (1894–1937) is another of the legendary women of the blues, and stories of her moxie abound—such as the one that claims she stood with hands on hips in defiance of a group of Klansmen who were seeking to tear down the tent where she was singing. At the same time, the story goes, she was shouting at her cowering stagehands, calling them "a bunch of sissies." Bessie Smith also auditioned for none other than Thomas Edison in 1924, who simply noted for his talent file that her voice was "n.g.," for "no good." The public had another opinion, however—"Down Hearted Blues," her first of many successful records, sold 750,000 copies, and she even appeared briefly on Broadway in 1929, in a revue entitled *Pansy*. In the same year, she starred in her only film, *St. Louis Blues*.

There is also the famous tale of the end of her life, which says she bled to death following an automobile accident, allegedly because no hospital would admit a black woman. In truth, the cause of her death appears to have been, in the words of writer

Francis Davis, "poor judgment, not racism." A white Memphis doctor by the name of Dr. Hugh Smith came upon the early morning wreck and placed Bessie Smith by the side of the road after sending for an ambulance. When the ambulance didn't show, the blues singer was loaded into Dr. Smith's car, but before they could leave for the hospital, another car driven by a drunken couple rammed into the doctor's vehicle. Two ambulances appeared on the scene and transported the injured. The couple who had plowed into Dr. Smith's car went to a white hospital, while Bessie Smith was taken to the hospital for blacks; however, only a quarter of a mile separated the two. The hit-and-run nature of the original accident combined with the second collision and the delayed arrival of the ambulance was enough to cause Bessie Smith to bleed to death.

I'm a hard working woman, baby,
I work hard sick or well.
But I can't stand my baby,
he's a heap of hell.

> MISSISSIPPI MATILDA
> *"Hard Working Woman"*

I'm as much woman as you are man.

> MARY DIXON
> *"Daddy, You Got Everything"*

It's all about a man
who always kicked and dogged me around.
And when I try to kill him,
that's when my love comes down.

> BESSIE SMITH
> *"Please Help Me Get Him
> off My Mind"*

Whoever said a good man was hard to find
positively, absolutely sure was blind.

> ETHEL WATERS
> *"My Handy Man"*

You never get nothing by being an angel child.
You better change your ways and get real wild,
'cause wild women don't worry.
Wild women don't have the blues.

> IDA COX
> *"Wild Women Don't Have
> the Blues"*

Sometime I believe trouble—and women—
are gonna take poor Lightnin' to his grave.

> LIGHTNIN' HOPKINS
> *"Tired of Trouble"*

He's a deep-sea diver
with a stroke that can't go wrong.
He can reach the bottom
'cause his breath holds out so long.

BESSIE SMITH
"Empty Bed Blues"

My baby won't talk to me
except to tell me nothing's wrong.

BRIAN ROBERTSON
"My Baby Won't Talk to Me"

I ask her where she's going,
she tells me where she's been.

MUDDY WATERS
"19 Years Old"

I ask for water, she bring me gasoline.

TOMMY JOHNSON
"Cool Drink of Water Blues"

I heard a rumbling sound deep in the ground.
It weren't a thing but the women trying to run me down.

BLIND SAMUEL
"Talking to Myself"

TOMMY JOHNSON

If you're a married man
you got no business here,
when you out with me.
I might make your wife shed tears.
I'm a mighty tight woman,
there is nothing I fear.

> SIPPIE WALLACE
> *"Mighty Tight Woman"*

Don't want no woman who wears a number nine.
I wake up in the morning, can't tell her shoes from mine.

> CHARLIE CAMBELL
> *"Going Away Blues"*

Little drops of water,
only grains of sand.
Every sensible woman
should have a backdoor man.

> SARA MARTIN
> *"Strange Lovin' Blues"*

A young man named Riley King traveled to radio station WDIA in Memphis in hopes of securing a radio program much like the one Sonny Boy Williamson II (Rice Miller) presided over at KWEM. He left the bus station and took a long walk through a heavy downpour, his guitar wrapped in a newspaper. Standing there sad-faced in the studio, this young, dripping wet musician began to play. The result? A fifteen-minute show sponsored by Paptikon, an elixir guaranteed to cure what ails you. Known as the Beale Street Blues Boy, his nickname was shortened to B. B. King.

Something 'bout your girlfriend I don't understand.
She cut off her hair now she looks like a man.
If that's what it takes to be hip,
I want you to be a square.
Don't want you messing around
and don't go cutting your hair.

> B. B. KING
> *"Don't Want You Cutting
> Your Hair"*

I don't want no woman if her hair ain't no longer than mine.

> LIGHTNIN' HOPKINS
> *"Short Haired Woman"*

I don't want no woman crazy about her processed hair.

> JOHN LEE HOOKER
> *"Processed"*

She got hair like a mermaid on the sea.
>> BLIND LEMON JEFFERSON
>> *"Stocking Feet Blues"*

Seems like you bald-headed women could show me a little hair sometime.
>> LIGHTNIN' HOPKINS
>> *"Bald Headed Woman"*

I got shined shoes and a nail manicure,
a diamond ring, man I got everything.
So don't you touch my head,
'cause I got a brand new process.
>> J. B. LENOIR
>> *"Don't Touch My Head"*

Samson thought Delilah was all on the square
till that little woman cut off all his hair.
>> GATEMOUTH BROWN
>> *"Ain't It Just Like a Woman?"*

Some of these women do make me tired.
Gotta handful of gimme, a mouthful of much obliged.
>> SLEEPY JOHN ESTES
>> *"Drop Down Mama"*

There are countless stories that talk about the love between a particular musician and his wife or lover. Many blues musicians suddenly found themselves on tour for the first time in their life, traveling far away from the places and people who were familiar to them. For that reason, it's not unusual to hear a blues singer singing about his or her missing love. In Lightnin' Hopkins's case, it was his lovely Little Antoinette. Mississippi Fred McDowell (1904–1972) often sang songs about missing his wife and worrying about her health when he recorded miles from home. Tampa Red (1904–1981) is another example of a blues singer whose love for his wife, Frances, literally kept him going.

Tampa Red was known as the Guitar Wizard because of his flawless bottleneck work on recordings with a variety of classic blues singers. His "Tight Like That" was a standard that cut across all boundaries of music as well as race and age. Tampa Red and Frances ran a kind of combination boarding house, rehearsal hall, and gabfest. After the death of his beloved wife, Tampa Red's mental and physical health deteriorated dramatically, and he died in 1981 in a psychiatric hospital—old, confused, and penniless.

She walks like she got oil wells in her backyard.

LIGHTNIN' HOPKINS
(title unknown)

If I had wings like an angel,
tell you where I would fly—
fly to the heart of Antoinette,
where poor Lightnin' would give up to die.

LIGHTNIN' HOPKINS
"So Sorry to Leave You"

The sun is going down,
moon begin to rise in blood.
Well, now life ain't worth living
if you ain't with the one you love.

JOHNNY TEMPLE
"The Sun Goes Down in Blood"

I ain't never loved
but three women in my life—
my mother, my sister,
and my partner's wife.

RAMBLIN' THOMAS
"Back Gnawing Blues"

I'd rather hear the screws in my coffin sound
rather than to hear my good gal say, "I'm jumpin' down."

FURRY LEWIS
"Furry's Blues"

FURRY LEWIS

Some long to have plenty money,
some want their wine and song.
All I crave is my sweet mama
that I dream about all night long.

>BARBECUE BOB
>*"Ease It to Me Blues"*

I done told you I love you,
what more can I do?

>BOBBY GRANT
>*"Nappy Head Blues"*

My woman's got teeth
like a lighthouse on the sea.
Every time she smiles,
she throws them lights on me.

>BILLY BIRD
>*"Down in the Cemetery"*

She's a tailor-made woman,
she ain't no hand-me-down.

>BLIND LEMON JEFFERSON
>*"Bad Luck Blues"*

What makes me love my baby?
She loved me when I was down.
She was nice and kind
and did not dog me around.
PEETIE WHEATSTRAW
"Good Woman Blues"

6th Street woman
you're like an angel in the night.
You give life to the dead,
give a blind man his sight.
With your long shapely legs
and those drop-dead eyes,
a man walking behind you
get some cardiovascular exercise.
BRIAN ROBERTSON
"6th Street Woman"

These women don't want that old halfway stuff.
So when you turn 'em loose, man,
be sure they got enough.
TAMPA RED
"You Got to Love Her with a Feeling"

You know I don't love you, baby,
but you're always resting on my mind.
                    MUDDY WATERS
                    "Standing Around Crying"

I'd walk through a blaze of fire
if I knew you were on the other side,
just to put my arms around you
to keep my love alive.
                    OTIS SPANN
                    "Burning Fire"

Love can make a poor man rich
or break his heart,
I don't know which.
                    MUDDY WATERS
                    "Forty Days and Forty Nights"

Jimmy Reed (1925–1976) had such a consistent sound
that it has been suggested he simply recorded one very long
song with hundreds of verses. That signature sound—the
walkup on the bass, the high notes from the harmonica, and
the lazy vocal style—is instantly recognizable in songs like

"Bright Lights, Big City" and "Big Boss Man." Reed's story is ultimately a tragic one. He was finally so affected by his intense alcoholism and epileptic seizures that he could not stand on stage for more than ten minutes at a time. At the time of his death he was preparing to attempt a comeback after having undergone treatment for the alcoholism that had ravaged him.

Much of Reed's success can be credited to his wife. Mary Lee "Mama" Reed authored a number of Jimmy Reed's twenty-two songs that made the charts in the U.S. It is also said that Mama Reed would whisper the lyrics in her husband's ear as he played and that she kept him going no matter how bad things got.

Have you ever loved a woman
better than you did yourself?

> LIGHTNIN' HOPKINS
> *"Have You Ever Loved
> a Woman?"*

Sometimes I'm broke and blue as I can be,
but still my baby looks after me.

> WILLIAM MOORE
> *"One Way Gal"*

I did more for you baby than you understand—
you can tell by the bullet holes here in my hand.

> PEETIE WHEATSTRAW
> *"Thinkin' and Worrying"*

It's hard to love someone
when that someone don't love you.

> ALBERTA HUNTER
> *"Down Hearted Blues"*

I think it's unfair to love and not be loved.
I think it means beware
when you kiss and cannot hug.

> WHISTLIN' ALEX MOORE
> *"Heart Wrecked"*

You know I'm wild about you, baby.
Wonder do you ever think of me?

> JOHN LEE HOOKER
> *"Think of Me"*

Further on up the road,
somebody gonna hurt you like you hurt me.

> MAGIC SLIM
> *"Further on up the Road"*

Now it's a pity and a shame,
the tricky actions of a woman's brain.
Soon as she find you want her and her only,
right away she go and make a change.

> MERCY DEE
> *"Pity and a Shame"*

Undertaker here and gone,
I gave him your height and size.
You'll be making whoopee with the devil
in hell tomorrow night.

> KING SOLOMON HILL
> *"Whoopee Blues"*

I believe I'll buy me a graveyard of my own.
I'm gonna kill everybody that have done me wrong.

> FURRY LEWIS
> *"Furry's Blues"*

I've been treated like an orphan
and been working like a slave.
If I never get my revenge,
evilness will carry me to my grave.

> WASHBOARD SAM
> *"I've Been Treated Wrong"*

Life ain't worth much if you ain't with the one you love.
BLIND BOY FULLER
"Lost Lover Blues"

They call me back-biter.
You might risk me, brother,
but I will never risk you.
If you allow me half a chance,
I will gnaw your backbone in two.
RAMBLIN' THOMAS
"Back Gnawing Blues"

You mistreated me
and you drove me away from your door.
But the good book says,
"You gonna reap just what you sow."
ALBERTA HUNTER
"Down Hearted Blues"

It may be a week,
and it may be a month or two.
All the dirt you doing to me
is coming back home to you.
ALBERTA HUNTER
"Down Hearted Blues"

RAMBLIN' THOMAS

I fold my arms and I walk away.
Your troubles will come some day.
SON HOUSE
"My Black Mama"

I'm so glad this whole round world do know
that every living creature reaps just what they sow.
TIM WILKINS
"Dirty Deal Blues"

I'm gonna make you wish you'd never been born.
I just went uptown and got my gun out of pawn.
HATTIE HART
"Papa's Got Your Water On"

I don't want to hurt that man,
just going to kill him dead.
MERLINE JOHNSON
(THE YAS YAS GIRL)
"Two by Four Blues"

Just like if you blue about something and you hear a good record you like. You don't play nothing but that record. Now say you if you have a girlfriend and she done gone off with some other boy,

*well you maybe go to the jukebox and have you some nickels in
your pocket. Well it's a certain record on that jukebox gonner
make you think about her. You ain't gonner play nothing but that
record. That's the way that go.*

> — JAMES THOMAS
> in *Blues from the Delta*,
> by William Ferris, Jr.

I was sitting here thinking, baby, just a minute ago.
What in the world made me love you so?

> WALTER DAVIS
> *"What Made Me Love You So?"*

Change in the ocean,
change in the deep blue sea.
Take me back, baby,
you'll find some change in me.

> SLEEPY JOHN ESTES
> *"Everybody Ought to Make
> a Change"*

BLUES AIN'T NOTHIN'
BUT SEX MISSPELLED

She stood on the corner
between Twenty-fifth and Main.
Well now a blind man saw her
and a dumb man called her name.

SLUEFOOT JOE
"Tooten Out Blues"

He's got to wake me every morning 'bout half past three,
kick up my furnace and turn on my heat.
Churn my milk, cream my wheat,
brown my biscuits, and chop my meat.

LIL JOHNSON
"Hottest Gal in Town"

Woman I'm loving,
she's long and tall.
Sleeps with her feet in the kitchen
and her head in the hall.

VARIOUS ARTISTS
(title unknown)

I want you to love me till the hair stands on my head.
>   MUDDY WATERS
>   *"I Want You to Love Me"*

Get your pan ready,
I'm gonna beat your bread.
>   LEE GREEN
>   *"I'm Gonna Beat Your Bread"*

Now I've been captain on this towboat
for twenty-eight years or more,
so just tell me how you want it
and I'll tow you 'cross the floor.
>   MERLINE JOHNSON
>   (THE YAS YAS GIRL)
>   *"Easy Towing Man"*

Alan Lomax, son of renowned folklorist John Lomax, documented countless examples of the blues for the Library of Congress. While on a journey to search for Robert Johnson (who Lomax did not know had already been murdered), Lomax discovered and recorded Muddy Waters. Perhaps one of Lomax's greatest finds was Son House. In his 1993 memoir *The Land Where Blues Began*, Lomax recalled:

"His voice, guttural and hoarse with passion, ripping apart

the surface of the music . . . while his powerful, work-hard hands snatched strange chords out of the steel strings. . . . And with him the sorrow of the blues was not tentative, or retiring, or ironic. Son's whole body wept, as with his eyes closed, the tendons in his powerful neck standing out with the violence of his feelings and his brown face flushing, he sang in an awesome voice the 'Death Letter Blues.'"

He treats me mean,
only comes to see me sometime,
but the way he spreads his honey,
makes me think I'll lose my mind.

> HATTIE NORTH
> *"Honey Dripper Blues"*

Take it easy, greasy,
love me till I get enough.

> LIL JOHNSON
> *"Take It Easy, Greasy"*

Hitch me to your buggy, baby,
drive me like a mule.

> BLIND LEMON JEFFERSON
> *"Rabbit Foot Blues"*

Big Joe Williams (1903–1982) was hired to play at a small club in London, and when a well-known blues writer showed up at the station, Big Joe was nowhere to be found. After two hours, the writer headed to the hotel where Big Joe was supposed to have checked in upon his arrival. The writer was greatly relieved to discover the bluesman had already arrived.

He found Big Joe lying on the bed in his room with a package of condoms on the table next to him.

"Where the hell have you been?" asked the writer.

"Forget that," Big Joe said. "Where the hell are the women?"

Loving night and day is the thing I crave.
Give me lots of loving and I'll be your slave.

> SARA MARTIN
> *"Strange Loving Blues"*

Lord, if you can't send me no woman,
send me a sissy man.

> PINEWOOD TOM (JOSH WHITE)
> *"Sissy Man"*

Run into me, but don't hurt me.

> LIL JOHNSON
> *"Never Let Your
> Left Hand Know"*

Hey baby, won't you cuddle near?
Let sweet mama whisper in your ear.
I'm wild about that thing.
It makes me laugh and sing.
Give it to me papa,
I'm wild about that thing.

> BESSIE SMITH
> *"I'm Wild About That Thing"*

Watch out little woman!
Big fat woman make a married man jump and shout!

> HOUND DOG TAYLOR
> *"Watch Out"*

Women loving each other,
they don't think about no man.
They ain't playing it secret no more,
these women playing a wide open hand.

> MEMPHIS WILLIE
> *(title unknown)*

If you can dish it out, I can take it.
I got to have it morning, noon, and night.

> LIL JOHNSON
> *"If You Can Dish It Out"*

I'm dynamite baby,
all you do is light my fuse.
With my eyes closed, baby,
I'm gonna blow away your blues.

SLIM HARPO
"Dynamite"

I dreamed last night I was far from harm,
woke up and found my man in a sissy's arms.
My man's got a sissy, his name is "Miss Kate."
He shook that thing like jelly on a plate.

MA RAINEY
"Sissy Blues"

I love you honey,
but your mother's gotta move.

BIG WALTER
(title unknown)

What she did to me, people,
ain't never been done before.
But she really made me like it,
and I want to do some more.

PEETIE WHEATSTRAW
"Block and Tackle"

BIG BILL BROONZY

So, take me pretty baby
and jump me in your big brass bed.
I want you to rock me, pretty baby,
till my face turns cherry red.
> BIG JOE TURNER
> *"Cherry Red"*

Your face is all hid
and your back's all bare.
If you ain't doing the hobo,
what's your head doing there?
> SPECKLED BIRD
> *"Dirty Dozens No. 2"*

Rock me baby, rock me all night long.
I want you to rock me baby,
like my back ain't got no bone.
> BIG BILL BROONZY
> *"Rock Me Baby"*

Ain't but one thing that makes me really sore—
when you grind me one time and just don't do it no more.
> DORTHEA TROWBRIDGE AND
> STUMP JACKSON
> *"Steady Grinding"*

Something to tell you
when I gets a chance.
I don't wanna marry,
just wanna be your man.

> CHARLEY PATTON
> *"Stone Pony Blues"*

THE BLUES BY ANY OTHER NAME

Nicknames and pseudonyms are an important feature of
the blues. Here are a few, along with the given names of
their owners. (It should be fairly easy to figure out that the
blues nicknames are the ones on the left!)

Kokomo Arnold	James Arnold
Barbecue Bob	Robert Hicks
Bumble Bee Slim	Amos Easton
Honeyboy Edwards	David Edwards
Jazz Gillum	William Gillum
Homesick James	James Williamson (aka John Henderson)

Honey Dripper	Roosevelt Sykes
Howlin' Wolf	Chester Burnett
Lil' Son Jackson	Melvin Jackson
Albert King	Albert Nelson
Furry Lewis	Walter Lewis
Lightnin' Slim	Otis Hicks
Little Walter	Marion Walter Jacobs
Louisiana Red	Iverson Minter
Ma Rainey	Gertrude Pridgett
Magic Sam	Samuel Maghett
Magic Slim	Morris Holt
Memphis Minnie	Lizzie Douglas
Memphis Slim	Peter Chatman
Mercy Dee	Mercy D. Walton
Muddy Waters	McKinley Morganfield
Robert Nighthawk	Robert McCollum or Robert Lee McCoy
Professor Longhair	Henry Roland "Roy" Byrd
Slim Harpo	James Moore
Sunnyland Slim	Albert Luandrew
Tampa Red	Hudson Whittaker

Hound Dog Taylor	Theodore Roosevelt Taylor
Koko Taylor	Cora Walton
T-Bone Walker	Aaron Walker
Washboard Sam	Robert Brown
Peetie Wheatstraw	William Bunch
Sonny Boy Williamson	John Lee Williamson
Sonny Boy Williamson, II	Aleck "Rice" Miller
The Yas Yas Girl	Merline Johnson

I left my little baby when she was only four days old.
I just hope she doesn't learn to call no other man "Daddy,"
you know, that's what's worrying me.

SONNY BOY WILLIAMSON
"Mean Old Highway"

Don't mistreat me
because I'm young and wild.
Sister, you ought to remember
that you once was a child.

BLIND LEMON JEFFERSON
"Stocking Feet Blues"

It may be funny, funny as can be.
We got eight children, baby,
don't none of them look like me.

BIG BILL BROONZY
"I'm Gonna Move"

I know I was born to die,
but I hate to leave my children crying.

BUKKA WHITE
"Fixin' to Die"

Motherless children have a hard time
when mother is dead.

BLIND WILLIE JOHNSON
"Motherless Children"

If you mistreat me,
you mistreat a mother's child.

FURRY LEWIS
"Big Chief Blues"

Oh daughter, daughter, please don't be like me.
You fall in love with every man you see.

ELVIE THOMAS
"Motherless Child Blues"

My stepfather treat me so mean,
he made my mother get on her knees.
She said if you hit my son again,
I'm gonna have to call the police.

HUDSON SHOWERS
"Rough Treatment"

You oughta understand your children.

LIGHTNIN' HOPKINS
"Got to Move Your Baby"

WHEN THE BACKDOOR SLAMS . . .

Cheating is one of the cornerstones of country-and-western music, and it's certainly one of the high-octane fuels that power the blues. One of the most talked about characters in blues has to be the infamous "backdoor man." His name comes from the way he flies out the back of the house as the husband walks in the front. The most famous tribute, "Back Door Man," was written by Willie Dixon and was brought to life by the great Howlin' Wolf in 1966.

Howlin' Wolf (Chester Burnett, 1910–1976) was one of the most astonishing characters in blues history. A hulking figure over six feet tall and weighing right at three hundred pounds, Howlin' Wolf was the stuff legends are made of. Whether enveloping the microphone, screaming and howling as if on the verge of exploding, or wiggling about on the floor as if in a hoodoo seizure, Wolf was the essence of Chicago Blues electric style. His rivalry with fellow Chess artist Muddy Waters (often competing for songs written by Dixon) caused both artists to rise to new heights.

If you don't give me what I want,
I'm gonna get it somewhere else.

LIL JOHNSON
"If You Don't Give Me What I Want"

Make me a pallet on your floor.
If you feel like lying down with me
on that pallet on the floor,
when your main gal come,
I swear, she will never know.

> MA YANCEY
> *"Make Me a Pallet
> on Your Floor"*

I am your back door man—
the women don't know,
but the little girls,
they understand.

> HOWLIN' WOLF
> *"Back Door Man"*

He came by me running,
smelling like a garbage can,
with one leg in his pants
and his shoes in his hand.

> CASEY BILL WELDON
> *"Back Door Blues"*

Can't no woman unbackdoor me
if I'm your one-and-all
or else your used-to-be.
>   EMERY GLEN
>   *"Backdoor Blues"*

I worked for you so many times
when I really was too sick to go.
I worked for you baby,
when your man was slippin' in my backdoor.
>   LONNIE JOHNSON
>   *"I'm Gonna Be Your Fool"*

Mississippi Fred McDowell emerged as a link to the past when recorded in the 1960s. His style was raw—a repetitive bottleneck riff against a rough, powerful vocal—but his influence has been surprisingly strong. The Rolling Stones covered his "You Got To Move," and much of Bonnie Raitt's slide guitar style can be traced back to McDowell's work. As for McDowell, he made his place in music clear, saying time and time again, "I don't play no rock and roll."

She won't shake her moneymaker.
>   ELMORE JAMES
>   *"Shake Your Moneymaker"*

I had a little girl, she was little and low.
She used to like to shake it,
but she don't no more.
Somebody's been using that thing.

> HOLMES AND HOWARD
> *"Somebody's Been Using
> That Thing"*

The copper brought her in,
she didn't need no bail.
She shook it for the judge
and they put the cop in jail.

> TAMPA RED
> *"No Matter How She Done It"*

What you got in mind
ain't gonna happen today.
Get off my bed.
How in the world did you get that way?

> MARY DIXON
> *"You Can't Sleep in My Bed"*

Another mule's kickin' in your stall.

> MUDDY WATERS
> *"Long Distance Call"*

The clock's on the shelf
going tick tick tick,
your mama's on the street
doin' I don't know which.

> VARIOUS ARTISTS
> *"Dirty Dozens"*

If you talk in your sleep,
please don't mention my name.

> BLIND WILLIE McTELL
> *(title unknown)*

My sweet mama got another man
rootin' around in her ash can.

> BOB CLIFFORD
> *"Ash Can Blues"*

My baby ran away with the garbage man.
Please come back to me honey,
so you can empty my garbage can.

> MUDDY WATERS
> *"Garbage Can Blues"*

Woman, your husband is cheating on us.

> UNKNOWN

When I catch a man with my woman
I usually tear his playhouse down.

> BIG MACEO MERRIWETHER
> *"Mace's 32-30"*

You can always tell
when your woman's got another man—
your meals ain't regular
and your home ain't never clean.

> BLIND BOY FULLER
> *(title unknown)*

Tell you this, men,
ain't gonna tell you nothing else.
Man's a fool if he thinks
he's got a woman to himself.

> BLIND WILLIE REYNOLDS
> *(title unknown)*

Too many dirty dishes
in the sink for just us two.
You got me wondering, baby—
who's making dirty dishes with you?

> ALBERT COLLINS
> *"Too Many Dirty Dishes"*

Don't tell nobody you saw me creepin' by —
she's got a mean old man and I don't want to die.

> JUKE BOY BONNER
> *"Running Shoes"*

My baby don't stand no cheating.
She don't like none of that midnight creeping.

> LITTLE WALTER
> *"My Baby"*

You can steal my chickens, boys,
but you sure can't make 'em lay.
You can steal my best woman,
but you sure can't make her stay.

> BIG JOE WILLIAMS
> *"Someday Baby"*

Moaning, groaning, groaning, phoning . . .
oh . . . there must be somebody there.
Central, Central, tell me that's what I hear.
Lord, could another woman be there?
So tired of walking the floor,
wringing my hands and pulling my hair.

> VICTORIA SPIVEY
> *"Telephoning the Blues"*

I started to kill my woman
till she lay down across the bed.
She looked so ambitious
till I took back everything I said.

WILLIE BROWN
"M & O Blues"

When my baby was here with me,
my telephone kept on ringing all the time.
But now, since she left me,
my telephone don't never ring.
That's why I know now people,
there was something going on.

JOHN LEE HOOKER
"Me and My Telephone"

Rather than see someone else mistreat you,
I'd rather keep you and mistreat you myself.

FUNNY PAPA SMITH
"Mama, Quittin' and Leaving"

THE THRILL IS GONE

In some relationships, there comes a day when everything's over. A blues fan told me late one night in a club after I'd finished playing, "You know what got me through my divorce? The blues. I suppose I must have played B. B. King's 'The Thrill Is Gone' two hundred and fifty times. My neighbors probably thought I was out of my mind—which I was. But each time I heard that song, I got a little stronger. What's it that John Lee Hooker says about the blues? 'It's a healer'—that's it, exactly!"

Used to be my sugar,
but you ain't sweet no more.
> SLUEFOOT JOE
> *"Tooten Out Blues"*

Sugar babe, I'm tired of you.
Ain't your honey but the way you do.
> MANCE LIPSCOMB
> *"Sugar Babe"*

The thrill is gone.
> B. B. KING
> *"The Thrill Is Gone"*

Sometimes I say I need you,
then again I don't.
Sometimes I think I'll quit you,
then again I won't.

CHARLEY PATTON
"Bird Nest Bound"

Woke up this morning
with the blues three different ways.
Had two minds to leave you,
only one to stay.

CHARLIE LINCOLN
"Depot Blues"

Sitting here thinking—
should I cry or let you go?
Little things we used to do,
we don't do no more.

OTIS SPANN
"Burning Fire"

I'm gonna miss you like the devil,
but these things I'll overcome.

SLIM HARPO
"Miss You Like the Devil"

C. C. Rider,
now see what you have done?
Made me love you,
now your man done come.

VARIOUS ARTISTS
"C. C. Rider"

Between midnight and dawn, baby,
we may ever have to part.
But there's one thing about it, baby,
please remember I've always been your heart.

JOHNNY TEMPLE
"Between Midnight and Dawn"

If I lose you darling,
I got to go and look for me another friend.

LIGHTNIN' HOPKINS
"My Suggestion"

If you can stand to leave me,
I'd just love to see you go.

SONNY BOY WILLIAMSON
"Western Union Man"

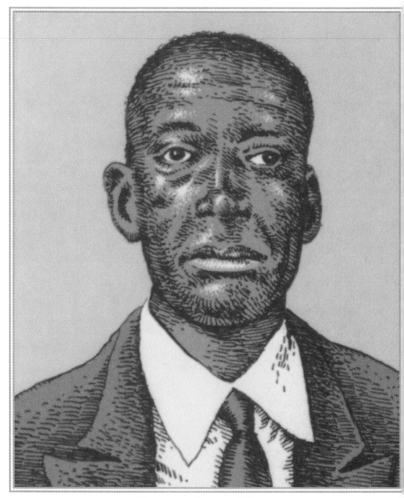

SLEEPY JOHN ESTES

Baby done quit me,
ain't said a mumblin' word.
It weren't nothing that she knowed of,
just something she had heard.
SLEEPY JOHN ESTES
"Stack O'Dollars Blues"

I'm going so far I can't hear your rooster crow.
FURRY LEWIS
"Dry Land Blues"

Give me back that wig I bought you,
give me back the one glass eye.
Give me back the teeth I loaned you,
baby don't you say good-bye.
When I take my pegleg,
you gonna fall right down and cry.
JOHNNY WINTER
"Give It Back"

Oh baby, you lost your good thing now.
You been foolin' me, I found out somehow.
MANCE LIPSCOMB
*"Tell Me Where You Stayed
Last Night"*

Good-bye pretty mama,
baby fare thee well.
Lord, I'm afraid to meet you
in that other world somewhere.

TIM WILKINS
"Dirty Deal Blues"

If I was cold and hungry,
I wouldn't even ask you for bread.
I don't want you no more,
if I'm on my dying bed.

LEROY'S BUDDY
"Triflin' Woman Blues"

My baby left town,
she left me a mule to ride.
When the train pulled out of the station,
that mule upped and died.

SONNY BOY WILLIAMSON
"Western Union Man"

You see my women went and left me
and now my mind is trying to leave me, too.

ALBERT COLLINS
"My Mind Is Leaving Too"

CANNON'S JUG STOMPERS

When I leave, I'll be running, dodging trees.
You'll see the bottom of my feet so many times
you'll think I'm on my knees.

> CANNON'S JUG STOMPERS
> *"Prison Wall Blues"*

T-Bone Walker (1910–1975) was a Texas bluesman who performed as a tap dancer in traveling medicine shows, worked in vaudeville, and crossed paths at an early age with blues legends Texas Alexander and Blind Lemon Jefferson. In addition, he spent some time playing banjo in Cab Calloway's band before becoming one of the very first blues players to use an electric guitar on a regular basis. His monster classic, "Stormy Monday Blues," alone would have been enough to ensure his fame in the annals of blues history. Walker crafted a sound that was light and jazzy but still true to the blues. His style of performing—guitar behind the head or between his legs, doing splits—echoes of Charley Patton—certainly influenced a number of younger musicians, from Chuck Berry to Jimi Hendrix.

I grabbed my pillow,
turned over in my bed.
I cried about my daddy
till my cheeks turned cherry red.

> MA RAINEY
> *"Victim of the Blues"*

There's nothing I can do
if you leave me here to cry,
but my love will follow you
as the years go passing by.

> ALBERT KING
> *"As the Years Go Passing By"*

This is a mean old world to live in by yourself.
> T-BONE WALKER
> *"Mean Old World"*

When you looked at me
I was about to cry.
Ain't gonna give up nothing
if I should die.
But old times will get you by and by.
> LIGHTNIN' HOPKINS
> *"Lonesome Lightnin'"*

I would have cried, baby,
what good would it do?
You couldn't have heard me
cry the doggone blues.
> J. B. HUTTO
> *"Now She's Gone"*

Yes, I'm going,
and your crying won't make me stay.
The more you cry, little woman,
the further you drive me away.
> JOHN LEE HOOKER
> *"Drive Me Away"*

You never had to cry,
don't start crying now.
You ain't never loved me,
didn't do me no good no how.
SLIM HARPO
"Don't Start Crying Now"

The sky is crying—
look at the tears rolling down the street.
ELMORE JAMES
"The Sky Is Crying"

My baby's leaving,
and crying won't make her stay.
If it would,
I'd cry myself away.
TOMMIE BRADLEY
"Window Pane Blues"

KEEP IT CLEAN

Not every relationship in the blues fails because of cheating. A few never get off the ground because of other problems, as witnessed by the fact that there are a few blues that double as public service announcements promoting personal hygiene.

Only one thing makes me mad—
breath smells like something the buzzards had.
CHAMPION JACK DUPREE
"You've Been Drunk"

You smell like a garbage can late at night.
BOOGIE BILL WEB
"Drinkin' and Stinkin'"

You're too big to be cute
and I don't think you're clean.
MARY DIXON
"You Can't Sleep in My Bed"

Now ride her on over, give her a Coca-Coly,
lemon sody, saucer of ice cream—
takes soap and water for to keep it clean.
CHARLIE JORDAN
"Keep It Clean"

When a man gets hairy,
know he needs a shave.
When a woman gets musty,
oh, you know she needs to bathe.
TEXAS ALEXANDER
"98 Degree Blues"

Mojos, Goofer Dust, and the
Root of the Blues

Woven through so much of the blues is the element of magic, manifested most notably in the infamous *mojo*. A mojo can take several forms in the blues. Sometimes it is used as a charm to keep a woman from getting another man (or vice versa, though not as often) or as a bit of extra magic to make a woman interested in a man. There are other forms of magic besides the mojo. Goofer or goober dust — dust taken from the grave of a child — is said to have magical properties. Also, from various combinations of roots, animal hair, ashes, and rocks are said to come good luck and wealth.

The most powerful of these magical aids would be the famous John the Conqueror Root, which must be collected before September 21 each year to be of value. To this day, stores in the South sell strange little jars that contain John the Conqueror Root — made, by the way, in Chicago.

In the mid-1800s the first hoodoo doctor in New Orleans was named Dr. John — the nickname also of a great New Orleans–style blues piano player of more modern times. A mind reader and astrologer, the original Dr. John was wildly successful. He was known for carrying around magical shells soaked in snake, frog, and lizard oil and wrapped in human hair that were purported to keep away evil. He was followed by other hoodoo doctors with colorful, evocative names such as Dr. Yah Yah and Dr. Jack. Dr. Jack's claim to fame was a unique magical charm—a beef heart he kept at the head of his bed. He declared that he would stay alive until (or unless) the heart touched the floor. It fell one day in 1868 and, true to his word, Dr. Jack died a few days later. After that came the legendary Dr. Beauregard, whose power was said to come from a hoot owl's head and from the magical paraphernalia he kept woven in tiny holders in his waist-length hair.

Well, I went to the gypsy
and I laid my money on the line.
I said, "Bring back my baby,
or please take her off my mind."

JOSHUA JOHNSON
"Gypsy Blues"

I know many of you men are wondering
what the snake doctor got in his hand.
He's got roots and herbs,
steals a woman everywhere he lands.

J. D. SHORT
"Snake Doctor Blues"

I'm gonna sprinkle a little goofer dust
all around your nappy head.
You'll wake up one of these mornings
and find you will be dead.

CHARLIE SPAND
"Big Fat Mama Blues"

My baby got a mojo
she won't let me see.
One morning about four o'clock
she eased that thing on me.

BLIND BOY FULLER
"Mojo Hiding Woman"

I call it black magic,
some call it plain hoodoo.

CURTIS JONES
"Black Magic Blues"

I believe my good gal
has found my black cat bone.
I can leave Sunday morning,
Monday morning I'm sitting back home.

BLIND LEMON JEFFERSON
"Broke and Hungry Blues"

I got me a mojo man, it sure is crazy.
But the gypsy forgot to tell me how to operate it.

> JOHNNY WINTER
> *"Mojo Boogie"*

I'm going to Louisiana,
get me a mojo hand.
Gonna fix my woman
so she can't have no other man.

> LIGHTNIN' HOPKINS
> *"Mojo Hand"*

Don't touch me with your broom,
don't let my lamp get low.
Don't let the dogs start to howling
'cause somebody got to go.

> JAZZ GILLUM
> *"The Blues What Am"*

Last night a hoot owl came
and sat right over my door.
A feeling seemed to tell me
I would never see my man no more.

> MA RAINEY
> *"Black Cat, Hoot Owl Blues"*

Somebody done hoodooed the Hoodoo Man.
>> SONNY BOY WILLIAMSON
>> *"Hoodoo Man Blues"*

I went to church, sat on the thirteenth row.
Next day my landlord said I had to go.
>> ELIZABETH SMITH
>> *"Going to Have Bad Luck*
>> *for Seven Years"*

It was midnight on a Sunday,
the clock struck thirteen times.
I was scared and I was frightened
because I sure believe this sign.
>> DOLLY ROSS
>> *"Hootin' Owl Blues"*

I got my mojo working,
but it just won't work on you.
>> MUDDY WATERS
>> *"Got My Mojo Working"*

Mama Don't Allow That
Boogie-Woogie 'Round Here

The blues was, plain and simple, considered to be the Devil's music. Robert Johnson and others capitalized on that belief, and because of this it was technically impossible for a blues lyric to call to God for assistance. For that reason, the blues became full of references to hoodoo as a means of seeking relief from problems. As for the word *hoodoo*, it appears to have been an alteration of the word *voodoo*, the change coming sometime in the early 1900s.

Black cat bones, for instance, are mentioned in the titles of songs by Lightnin' Hopkins, Thomas Dorsey, Peter Chatman, Bukka White, and Brownie and Sonny. *Hoodoo* shows up in tunes by Lightnin' Slim, Dave Alexander, Junior Wells, Victoria Spivey, Tabby Thomas, Johnny Temple, and Sonny Boy Williamson. Mojos are found in songs by Muddy Waters, Walter Davis, Lightnin' Hopkins, and Ida Cox.

While popular religion had its opinion about the blues, the blues had an opinion about the ways of the church. There was more than a little skepticism and cynicism on the part of the bluesmen and -women about the sincerity of preachers, deacons, and members of the choir.

Oh, I'm gonna get me religion,
I'm gonna join the Baptist church.
I'm gonna be a Baptist preacher,
and I sure won't have to work.

> SON HOUSE
> *"Preachin' the Blues"*

If you want to see a preacher cuss,
bake the bread, sweet mama,
and save him the crust.

> HI HENRY BROWN
> *"Preacher Blues"*

What makes a man go crazy
when a woman puts on that evening gown?
It's the same old thing
made a preacher throw his Bible down.

> WILLIE DIXON
> *"Same Old Thing"*

My mother told me, "Son, don't forget to pray."
I fell down on my knees, I forgot just what to say.

> LIGHTNIN' HOPKINS
> *"Baby"*

FRANK STOKES

Church bell's a'ringing, preacher's preaching,
secretary's writing, the members shouting.
The dirty deacon has taken my gal and gone.

RUBE LACY
"Ham Hound Cave"

Oh, well, it's our Father who art in Heaven—
the preacher owed me ten dollars, he paid me seven.
Thy kingdom come, thy will be done—
if I hadn't taken the seven, Lord,
I wouldn't have gotten none.

FRANK STOKES
"You Shall"

There were many musicians who moved from blues to gospel—changing sides, as it were. Some switched back and forth a few times. Even though Leadbelly "got religion," this didn't keep him from playing dances—a fact that caused some friction with the church. Leadbelly's reaction? "The church people raise more hell than any twenty people I ever seen."

The legendary Son House (1902–1988) was a preacher until one day he walked away from the church after hearing a blues tune being played on a slide guitar. He went on to produce some devastating blues, perhaps the greatest examples of Delta style that can be found. One of the most powerful influences on Robert Johnson, Son House's music is a perfect example of the ability of the blues to give a voice to the darker side of life. His classic "Preachin' the Blues" is a brilliant example of the conflicts between the secular and the sacred.

You snuff dippers, tobacco chewers—
when you get to heaven, you won't have nowhere to spit.

SISTER O. M. TERRELL
"The Bible's Right"

Ain't no heaven, ain't no burnin' hell.
When I die, where I go can't nobody tell.

JOHN LEE HOOKER
"Burnin' Hell"

You know, this must be the Devil I'm serving.
I know it can't be Jesus Christ.
'Cause I asked him to save me
and it looks like he's trying to take my life.

FUNNY PAPA SMITH
(title unknown)

I wish I had me a heaven of my own.
Well, I'd give all my women a long, long happy home.

SON HOUSE
"Preachin' the Blues"

Don't let the devil steal the beat from the Lord!
MAHALIA JACKSON
(title unknown)

Oh, I got to stay on the job,
I ain't got no time to lose.
I swear to God,
I got to preach these gospel blues.
SON HOUSE
"Preachin' the Blues"

Willie Dixon (1915–1992) was an extremely important figure in the blues, doing just about everything that could be done at Chess Records—writer, recording-session bass player, singer, producer, talent scout. His work served as a kind of bridge into rock and roll—and not just through the countless rock covers of his songs such as "Little Red Rooster," "Spoonful," "You Shook Me," "Hoochie Coochie Man," "Seventh Son," and "You Can't Judge a Book by Its Cover." The link to rock and roll was very direct, since Dixon played on several Chuck Berry songs in the 1950s.

In his younger days he was a fighter who sparred with Joe Louis, but his career in the ring was cut short after only a few fights because he and his manager came to blows in the boxing commissioner's office. In 1941 Dixon landed in jail for refusing to go to war, after proclaiming his status as a conscientious objector.

Dixon later founded the Blues Heaven Foundation, Inc., to help spread recognition and acknowledgment of the blues. The foundation purchased the Chess Records building and continues to work in areas such as the offering of a Muddy Waters Scholarship and the donation of musical instruments to elementary and secondary schools.

I ain't superstitious,
but a black cat just crossed my trail.

> WILLIE DIXON
> *"I Ain't Superstitious"*

What makes a man go crazy
when a woman wears her dress so tight?
Same old thing make a tomcat fight all night.

> WILLIE DIXON
> *"Same Old Thing"*

I got a black cat bone, I got a mojo too,
I'm John the Conqueror, I'm gonna mess with you.

> WILLIE DIXON
> *"I'm Your Hoochie Coochie Man"*

Just a little spoon of your precious love satisfies my soul.
>WILLIE DIXON
>*"Spoonful"*

I was an innocent child till you taught me your style.
>WILLIE DIXON
>*"Whatever I Am You Made Me"*

MORE BLUES LEFT THAN YEARS
TO LIVE THEM

You're like an old horseshoe
that's had its day.
You're like an old shoe
I must throw away.

IDA COX
"Worn Out Daddy Blues"

Mama say when I was a baby, prettiest thing she had.
That's what remains of things in the past.
Baby, this ain't me.
I got so old, I don't even know myself.

ROBERT PETE WILLIAMS
"I Got So Old"

An old man ain't nothing
but a young woman's slave.
They work hard all the time trying
to stay in these young men's ways.

BLIND WILLIE REYNOLDS
"Nehi Blues"

All you young women ought to be ashamed—
taking these old men's money
when they walking on walking canes.
> BLIND WILLIE REYNOLDS
> *"Nehi Blues"*

Uncle Ned, you can't do the things you did years ago.
You remember you're ninety-four,
you can't shake that thing no more.
> UNKNOWN
> *"Uncle Ned"*

You ought to have heard my grandmother
when she got my grandfather told.
She said get away from me, man,
I swear you done got too old.
> SONNY BOY WILLIAMSON
> *"Shotgun Blues"*

If I could be young and stupid
or old and dumb,
I'd shake off the years
and you'd see me run.
> UNKNOWN

I'm too old for the orphanage
and too young for the old folks' home.

> WASHBOARD SAM
> *"I've Been Treated Wrong"*

I have had my fun if I don't get well no more.

> SUNNYLAND SLIM
> *"I Have Had My Fun"*

I wonder what made grandpa love your grandma so?
She got the same sweet jelly roll he had forty years ago.

> ED BELL
> *"Hambone Blues"*

Some people tell me
that God takes care of old folks and fools.
But since I was born,
he must have changed the rules.

> FUNNY PAPA SMITH
> *"Fool's Blues"*

You gonna look just like a monkey when you get old.

> HAMMIE NIXON
> *"You Gonna Look Just Like a
> Monkey When You Get Old"*

BACK TO MOTHER EARTH

The subject of death adds a strange texture to the blues, flavored by the sad fate of so many of the bluesmen and -women. Robert Johnson's poisoning is only one example. There are countless others.

Blind Lemon Jefferson (1897–1929) died in the bitter cold of a Chicago snowstorm after leaving a recording session for a party where he was scheduled to play. Some say he had a heart attack and died covered in snow, his guitar by his side. Others say he died waiting for his driver to arrive or that he simply became lost, sat down to play his guitar, and froze to death. No matter what the truth, Jefferson's most poignant thoughts about death are found in his lyrics, including his famous line, "There's one kind favor I'll ask of you—see that my grave is kept clean." Indeed, Jefferson was buried in Texas in the town of Wortham and for years lay in an unmarked, unkept grave.

Have my picture taken,
gonna have it put in a frame.
When I'm dead and gone,
you can see poor Lewis just the same.

JOHNNY LEWIS
"My Little Gal"

She stalks my pillow,
graveyard gonna be my bed.
Blue skies gonna be my blanket
and the pale moon gonna be my friend.

RED NELSON
"Crying Mother Blues"

You got to go down.

REVEREND GARY DAVIS
"You Got to Go Down"

Death is awful.
Spare me over another year.

DOC REED
"Death Is Awful"

It ain't no heaven and it ain't no burning hell.
Where I'm going when I die, can't nobody tell.

SON HOUSE
"My Black Mama"

What you gonna do
when death comes creepin' at your room?

MANCE LIPSCOMB
*"What You Gonna Do When Death Comes
Creepin' at Your Room?"*

REVEREND GARY DAVIS

Can't tell my future, can't tell my past.
It seems like every minute sure gonna be my last.

WILLIE BROWN
"Future Blues"

Don't bring me no flowers after I'm dead,
a dead man sure can't smell.
And if I don't go to heaven,
I sure won't need no flowers in hell.

PEETIE WHEATSTRAW
*"Bring Me Flowers
While I'm Living"*

When I die I want you to bury my body low,
just so that my evil spirit won't be
hanging around your door no more.

JOHN HENRY BARBEE
"Six Week Old Blues"

You know every loving creeper man was born to die.
But when that chariot come for you,
they gonna break, run, and try to hide.

LIGHTNIN' HOPKINS
"Death Bells"

BARBECUE BOB

You so beautiful,
but you got to die some day.
All I want is some loving
just before you pass away.

JOE TURNER
"Roll 'em Pete"

INFAMOUS BLUES DEATHS

Johnny Ace	Russian roulette during the intermission of a Christmas show in Houston
Barbecue Bob	Pneumonia and tuberculosis at age 29
Scrapper Blackwell	Shot to death in an alley in Indianapolis
Son Bonds	Accidentally shot
Juke Boy Bonner	Cirrhosis of the liver
Paul Butterfield	Drug-related heart attack

Leroy Carr	Acute alcoholism
Blind Boy Fuller	Blood poisoning
Jazz Gillum	Shot
Guitar Slim	Pneumonia at age 32
Earl Hooker	Tuberculosis at age 40
Freddy King	Bleeding ulcers, heart failure at age 42
Leadbelly	Lou Gehrig's disease
J. B. Lenoir	Car wreck and resultant heart attack at age 38
Meade Lux Lewis	Car wreck
Little Walter	Coronary thrombosis at age 37
Jimmy Reed	Alcoholism
Bessie Smith	Bled to death in car accident
Pine Top Smith	Accidentally shot at age 25 by a stray bullet from a barroom fight
Muddy Waters	Heart attack in his sleep at age 68
Peetie Wheatstraw	Auto accident at age 39

Please Mister, don't shoot me no more.
My breath is getting short
and my heart is beating awful slow.

SONNY BOY WILLIAMSON
"Bad Luck Blues"

Now when I'm dead, baby, don't you cry over me.
I'm trying to get back to my used-to-be.

GEORGIA PINE BOYS
"World's a Hard Place"

I don't care how rich you are,
don't care what you're worth.
When it all comes down,
you gotta go back home to Mother Earth.

MEMPHIS SLIM
"Mother Earth Blues"

I went to the cemetery,
look down in my baby's face.
Said I love you, baby,
but I sure can't take your place.

BILLY BIRD
"Down in the Cemetery"

I went down to Death Valley,
nothin' but tombstones and dry bones.
That's where a poor man be, Lord,
when I'm dead and gone.
>> ARTHUR "BIG BOY" CRUDUP
>> *"Death Valley Blues"*

Daddy, oh daddy, won't you answer me please?
All day I stood by your coffin
trying to give my poor heart ease.
>> IDA COX
>> *"Coffin Blues"*

When the Lord gets ready,
you got to move.
>> MISSISSIPPI FRED MCDOWELL
>> *"You Got to Move"*

Don't send no doctor,
he can't do me no good.
It's all my fault, mama,
I didn't do the things I should.
>> MANCE LIPSCOMB
>> *"Going Down Slow"*

I want you to remember this world don't last forever
and when you die, that is your end.

LIGHTNIN' HOPKINS
"Take It Easy, Baby"

I got one foot in the grave,
I gave a great big shout:
"St. Peter I can't go tonight,
we got a brand new rockin' sockin' record out!"

SLIM HARPO
"The Music's Hot"

I wish I knew how much life was mine.

LOTTIE BEAMAN
"Red River Blues"

Goin' out of this world someplace.

MANCE LIPSCOMB
"Goin' Down Slow"

I've looking funny in my eyes.
I believe I'm fixin' to die.

BUKKA WHITE
"Fixin' to Die"

A WORD OF ADVICE

It seems inappropriate to leave this book while talking about death, since so much of the blues is about life. With this in mind, it's important to recall that one of the other basic sources of the blues is the West African tradition known as *griot*. The word seems to be used in several ways: In one sense, a griot is a singer, while in another the word means a tribe's musical archives or libraries, which capture and present its history and culture. In essence, these songs and singers pass on vast amounts of wisdom from one generation to another, a tradition that continues in the advice offered by the blues.

Blues had a baby
and they named it rock 'n' roll.
                    MUDDY WATERS
                    "Blues Had a Baby"

Preacher told me that God'll forgive a black man
most anything he do.
I ain't black, but I'm dark complexioned,
look like you ought to forgive me, too.
                    FUNNY PAPA SMITH
                    "Howlin' Wolf Blues"

BLIND WILLIE McTELL

Take my advice:
Let those married woman be.
'Cause their husbands'll grab you,
beat you ragged as a cedar tree.

> BLIND WILLIE MCTELL
> *"Searching the Desert*
> *for the Blues"*

Hey everybody, let's have some fun.
You only live once
and when you're dead, you're gone.
So let the good times roll.

> KOKO TAYLOR
> *"Good Times"*

Never let your left hand know what your right hand do.

> LIL JOHNSON
> *"Never Let Your*
> *Left Hand Know"*

Be careful with a fool.
You know one day he may get smart.

> JOHNNY WINTER
> *"Be Careful with a Fool"*

Don't let a woman know you love her.
If you do, you have done wrong.
You come in from your work,
now she got her clothes and gone.

ARTHUR PETTIES
"Out on Santa Fe Blues"

If you get you one old woman,
you'd better get you five or six
so that if one happen to quit you
it won't leave you in an awful fix.

BLIND LEMON JEFFERSON
"Awful Fix"

Ain't it nice to be nice when you can be nice?

JIM JACKSON
*"Heard the Voice
of a Pork Chop Sing"*

You mix ink with water,
you bound to turn it black.
You run around with "funny" people,
you'll get a streak running up your back.

GEORGE HANNAH
"Freakish Blues"

You've got to live and let live,
you have to give and take.
You have to make-believe,
you have to pardon me.

BUMBLE BEE SLIM
"You Have to Live and Let Live"

When a man gets troubled in mind
he wants to sleep—all the time.
He knows if he can sleep all the time,
his troubles won't worry his mind.

BUKKA WHITE
"Sleepy Man's Blues"

If you gonna love your woman,
love her with a thrill.
If you don't,
you know some other man will.

TAMPA RED
"You've Got to Love Her with a Feeling"

It don't pay nobody to live this life fast.
Just take it slow and easy as long as it will last.

BUMBLE BEE SLIM
"Fast Life Blues"

ROOSEVELT SYKES

FINDING THE BLUES

There has never been so much information available on the blues, thanks to a number of factors including the rerelease of old material on CDs, the popularity of the blues in nightclubs and at festivals, and the dedicated band of blues fans on the Internet.

If you enjoyed the *Little Blues Book*, you might consider tracking down the original recordings, supporting blues music in your community, and making a place on your bookshelf for these and other references on the blues:

RECOMMENDED BOOKS

Calt, Stephen, and Gayle Wardlow. *King of the Delta Blues: The Life and Music of Charlie Patton*. Newton, N.J.: Rock Chapel Press, 1988.

Charters, Sam. *The Blues Masters*. New York: Da Capo Press, 1991.

———. *The Country Blues*. New York: Da Capo Press, 1975.

———. *The Legacy of the Blues*. New York: Da Capo Press, 1977.

Cohn, Lawrence. *Nothing but the Blues*. New York: Abbeville Press, 1993.

Dance, Helen Oakly. *Stormy Monday: The T-Bone Walker Story*. New York: Da Capo Press, 1990.

Davis, Francis. *The History of the Blues: The Roots, the Music, the People from Charley Patton to Robert Cray*. New York: Hyperion, 1995.

Evans, David. *Big Road Blues*. New York: Da Capo Press, 1987.

Ferris, William, Jr. *Blues from the Delta*. London: Studio Vista, 1970.

Garon, Paul. *The Devil's Son-in-Law: The Story of Peetie Wheatstraw and His Songs*. London: Studio Vista, 1971.

Guralnick, Peter. *Listener's Guide to the Blues*. New York: Facts on File, 1982.

———. *Lost Highway*. New York: Vintage Books, 1982.

———. *Searching for Robert Johnson*. New York: E. P. Dutton, 1989.

Hadley, Frank John. *The Grove Press Guide to the Blues on CD*. New York: Grove Press, 1993.

Harris, Sheldon. *Blues Who's Who*. New York: Da Capo Press, 1981.

Lipscomb, Mance. *I Say Me for a Parable: The Oral Autobiography of Mance Lipscomb, Texas Bluesman, as Told to and Compiled by Glyn Alyn*. New York: W. W. Norton and Company, 1993.

Lomax, Alan. *The Land Where Blues Began*. New York: Pantheon Books, 1993.

Mitchell, George. *Blow My Blues Away*. Baton Rouge, La.: Louisiana State University Press, 1971.

Morgan, Thomas L., and William Barlow. *From Cakewalks to Concert Halls*. Washington, D.C.: Elliot and Clark, 1992.

Obrecht, Jas, ed. *Blues Guitar*. San Francisco: Miller Freeman, 1993.

Oliver, Paul. *Blues Fell This Morning: The Meaning of the Blues*. Cambridge, Eng.: Cambridge University Press, 1990.

———. *Conversation with the Blues*. New York: Horizon Press, 1965.

Palmer, Robert. *Deep Blues*. New York: Penguin Books, 1981.

Pearson, Barry Lee. *Sounds Good to Me*. Philadelphia, Pa.: University of Pennsylvania Press, 1984.

Sackheim, Eric. *The Blues Line: A Collection of Blues Lyrics*. Hopewell, N.J.: Ecco Press, 1993.

RECOMMENDED MAGAZINES

Blues Access, 1514 North Street, Boulder, CO 80304

Juke Blues, P.O. Box 148, London W9 1 DY, England

Living Blues, Sam Hall, Rebel Drive, University of Mississippi, University, MS 38677

RECOMMENDED INTERNET RESOURCES

USENET GROUPS
rec.music.bluenote.blues
bit.listserv.blues-1

WORLD WIDE WEB Sites
Just point your favorite search engine toward "blues" and see the amazing number of sites that pop up. Some you might want to start with include:

BluesWEB — http://www.island.net/~blues/index.html

Blues-Links — http://transport.com/~firm/links.html

The Blue Highway — http://www.vivanet.com/~blues/links.html

The Blue List — http://www.hell-blues.nt.no/TheBlueList.html

Cascade Blues Association:— http://www.teleport.com/~boydroid/blues/links.htm

Blues Heaven Foundation — http://www.island.net/~blues/heaven.html

Living Blues — http://imp.cssc.oldmiss.edu/blues.html

Brian Robertson — http://www.realtime.net/~bluesman

AFTERWORD

It is my sincere hope that this book will inspire you to find the original recordings and support the countless small record companies that are busy reissuing the best of the old blues on CD. I write this knowing that once you've been bitten by the blues you'll be hooked, and you'll find yourself joyfully traveling its great river of wisdom and feeling. It can bring clarity and support to your life, and the discoveries that you will make about yourself and others will be among the most therapeutic and reassuring you'll be privileged to enjoy.

The development of the Internet allowed me to work with and share stories with blues lovers all over the world. I appreciate those who helped suggest lyrics and who pointed me in the right direction in terms of tracking down credits.

I am fortunate to have worked with three people who were extremely important in helping this project come together. The first is Rob Odom at Algonquin Books, who was there to get the thing started. I also want to thank Memsy Price at Algonquin for her editorial skills, her enthusiasm, and her sensitivity to the spirit and intent of this book. In the same way, Chris Stamey offered invaluable support in his comments, suggestions, and knowledge of the blues.

Finally, to dedicate this book is not difficult. I want to thank the incredible musicians—friends—I have played with over the years and also the audiences who have let me connect with them through my music. I also want to thank Shirley for her friendship and support as I worked over the past year to put this book together.

I am grateful for this chance also to thank my children for their understanding and for their love and support. I hope that in some small way, by my word or deed, I have given them a sense of what it means to have a dream in life, a calling, and then to follow it. While my calling has been the voice of the blues, theirs will most certainly be something different—but something found in the same place within their own hearts.

Finally, I would like to say that this book is primarily for those who helped create the music represented within these pages, the remarkable lives I've only touched on here. Their blues gives you, the reader and (I hope) listener, a chance to be touched by what they sang so many years ago and so many miles away, an eerie and yet oddly comforting experience. The connection that is created by the blues can make us realize that our deepest and most powerful feelings don't serve to keep us separate from each other, but rather bring us together as a part of what it means to be human, to be alive.

PERMISSIONS

LYRICS

"Back Door Man," written by Willie Dixon. © 1961, 1989 Hoochie Coochie Music (BMI)/Administered by Bug Music, Inc. All rights reserved. Used by permission.

"Be Careful with a Fool" (Joe Josea/Riley B. King), © 1985 Powerforce Music/Careers–BMG Music Publishing (BMI). All rights reserved. Used by permission.

"Big Boss Man," written by Mance Lipscomb. © 1971 Tradition Music (BMI)/Administered by Bug Music, Inc. All rights reserved. Used by permission.

"Blow Wind Blow," written by Muddy Waters. © 1969 Watertoons Music (BMI)/Administered by Bug Music, Inc./Arc Music. All rights reserved. Used by permission.

"Born Under a Bad Sign," written by William Bell and Booker T. Jones, Jr. © 1967, (renewed) 1970 East/Memphis Music Corp. Copyright assigned 1982 to Irving Music. All rights reserved. Used by permission.

"Crazy Mixed Up World," written by Willie Dixon. © 1959, 1987 Hoochie Coochie Music (BMI)/Administered by Bug Music, Inc. All rights reserved. Used by permission.

"Got My Mojo Working," written by Preston Foster. © 1956 by Preston Foster. Administered by Dare Music. All rights reserved. Used by permission.

"I Think I Got the Blues," written by Willie Dixon. © 1974 Hoochie Coochie Music (BMI)/Administered by Bug Music, Inc./Arc Music. All rights reserved. Used by permission.

"It Don't Make Sense (You Can't Make Peace)," written by Willie Dixon. © 1982 Hoochie Coochie Music (BMI)/Administered by Bug Music, Inc. All rights reserved. Used by permission.

"Lady Luck," written by Mercy Dee Walton. © 1970 Tradition Music (BMI)/Administered by Bug Music, Inc. All rights reserved. Used by permission.

"Long Distance Call," written by Muddy Waters. © 1959, 1987 Watertoons Music (BMI)/Administered by Bug Music, Inc. All rights reserved. Used by permission.

"Nobody Loves Me but My Mother," words and music by B. B. King. © 1970 by Sounds of Lucille, Inc. and Duchess Music Corporation. All rights controlled by Duchess Music Corporation, an MCA company. International copyright secured. All rights reserved. Used by permission.

"No Escape from the Blues," written by Muddy Waters and Charles Edward Williams. © 1959,

TEXT

For further information on blues music, please contact the Blues Heaven Foundation, 2120 S. Michigan Avenue, Chicago, IL 60616. (312)-808-1286.

CODA

Hurry down sunshine,
see what tomorrow brings.
May bring drops of sorrow,
it may bring drops of rain.

LEROY CARR
"Hurry Down Sundown"

There's a river somewhere
flows through the life of everyone.
And it flows around the mountains,
down through the meadows under the sun.

J. C. BURRIS
"River of Life"

Did I miss one of your favorite quotes or anecdotes? If so, please take the time to ship them in my direction. Be sure to include the source of the quote—a specific record, artist, etc. You can send it to me in care of Algonquin Books, P. O. Box 2225, Chapel Hill, NC 27515.

Shirley Allender

ABOUT THE AUTHOR

A native Texan and full-time musician, Brian Robertson plays the blues in Austin. He has worked as a radio talk show host, a museum director, a bus-boy, and a phone crisis hotline counselor. He has contributed articles to a number of magazines, including *Men's Health* and *Austin Blues Monthly*. His most recent CD release is *Juke Joint Blues*.

ABOUT THE ILLUSTRATOR

R. Crumb is one of the world's most celebrated cartoonists. His illustrations have appeared in numerous books and magazines over the past thirty years, and he's widely known as the creator of such characters as Fritz the Cat. He was recently the subject of Terry Zwigoff's acclaimed documentary film *Crumb*.